Trenton

ATLANTIC OCEAN

MAP OF THE

JERSEY SHORE

NEW JERSEY, USA

D1472136

THE
JERSEY SHORE
COOKBOOK

THE

JERSEY SHORE

COOKBOOK

FRESH SUMMER FLAVORS
FROM THE BOARDWALK AND BEYOND

DEBORAH SMITH

PHOTOGRAPHY BY THOMAS ROBERT CLARKE

QUIRK BOOKS

PHILADELPHIA

Library of Congress Cataloging in Publication Number: 2015946940

ISBN: 978-1-59474-872-1

Printed in the United States of America
Typeset in Kansas Casual, Maritime Champion, and Mr Eaves Sans

Designed by Andie Reid
Cover photo © Joerg Hackemann/Veer and Thomas Robert Clarke
Production management by John J. McGurk

Quirk Books
215 Church Street
Philadelphia, PA 19106
quirkbooks.com

10 9 8 7 6 5 4 3 2

This book is dedicated to the hardworking business owners who pour their hearts and souls into making the Jersey Shore a magical place.

CONTENTS

STARTERS AND SIDES

32
ALLAGASH STEAMERS
Marie Nicole's, *Wildwood Crest*

34
**JUMBO LUMP CRAB CAKES
WITH CHILI REMOULADE AND
JERSEY TOMATOES**
Chef Mike's ABG, *South Seaside Park*

36
BRIE EN CROÛTE
The Mad Batter Restaurant, *Cape May*

38
CAJUN SHRIMP AND GRITS
Brickwall Tavern and Dining Room, *Asbury Park*

43
OYSTERS GRATINÉE
Fratello's Restaurant, *Sea Girt*

SOUPS AND SALADS

48
CREAMY CRAB SOUP
Marie's Seafood, *Sea Isle City*

51
NEW ENGLAND CLAM CHOWDER
The Shrimp Box, *Point Pleasant Beach*

54
ROASTED TOMATO AND BASIL SOUP
Langosta Lounge, *Asbury Park*

58
SPICED CORN CHOWDER
Remington's, *Manasquan*

62
**CHILLED ROASTED NEW JERSEY
SWEET CORN AND BUTTERMILK SOUP**
Louisa's Café, *Cape May*

64
WATERMELON GAZPACHO
My Kitchen Witch, *Monmouth Beach*

66
BEACH PLUM FARM SALAD
The Ebbitt Room, *Cape May*

68
THE DIVING HORSE TOMATO SALAD
The Diving Horse, *Avalon*

70
**CHARRED JERSEY TOMATO SALAD
WITH SWEET CORN, ASPARAGUS TIPS,
AND HERB YOGURT**
Iron Room Restaurant, *Atlantic City*

72
**DUNGENESS CRAB SALAD
WITH LEMON VINAIGRETTE**
Avenue, *Long Branch*

77
**GRILLED TUNA NIÇOISE SALAD
WITH DIJON-THYME VINAIGRETTE**
Black-Eyed Susans, *Harvey Cedars*

80
JERSEY PEACH, HEIRLOOM TOMATO, AND LOBSTER SALAD WITH PEACH DRESSING
Ama Ristorante at Driftwood, *Sea Bright*

82
WATERMELON, SPINACH, AND BRANDIED PECAN SALAD
Waypoint 622, *Brielle*

MAIN COURSES

86
JERSEY COAST GRILLED BLUEFISH
Bahrs Landing, *Highlands*

91
TRASH CAKES AND FANCY SLAW
Quahog's Seafood Shack, *Stone Harbor*

95
VIKING VILLAGE SWORDFISH WITH PURPLE STICKY RICE, MAITAKE MUSHROOMS, AND MUSHROOM KOMBU DASHI
The Arlington, *Ship Bottom*

98
ISLAND TIME FISH TACOS
Jon and Patty's Coffee Bar and Bistro, *Ocean City*

102
PAN-SEARED NEW JERSEY BLACK SEA BASS WITH WHITE PEACH, TOMATO, AND BASIL SALSA
Shore Fresh Seafood, *Point Pleasant Beach*

106
PECAN-CRUSTED SALMON
Dock's Oyster House, *Atlantic City*

108
FLOUNDER OVES
Oves Restaurant, *Ocean City*

111
NEW JERSEY SKATE WITH SUMMER VEGETABLE RATATOUILLE
The Blue Pig Tavern, *Cape May*

115
PAN-SEARED NEW JERSEY TILEFISH WITH BACON CORN SUCCOTASH AND BASIL OIL
Beach Tavern, *Monmouth Beach*

118
GOLDEN TILEFISH SANDWICH
Joe's Fish Co., *Wildwood*

120
XXL BLTA
Sammy D's, *Atlantic City*

122
THE BLUEBERRY JACK BUBBA DOG WITH NEW JERSEY BLUEBERRY BBQ SAUCE
Bubba Dogs, *Sea Isle City*

124
LOBSTER ROLL
Brandl, *Belmar*

126
LOBSTER CEVICHE AND TOSTONES
The Red Store, *Cape May Point*

SANDY
WATER LINE
2012

INTRODUCTION

More than 59 million people call the Jersey Shore their vacation destination every year. I call it home.

My roots were planted in the sand of Sea Bright, New Jersey, well before I was born, when my grandfather founded the Tradewinds Beach Club and later became part owner of Surfrider Beach Club. He had a house directly across the street from Surfrider, and that's where I spent my summers, fishing in the Shrewsbury River and boogie boarding in the Atlantic Ocean.

I now live in Point Pleasant Beach, one of New Jersey's major vacation towns, about half a mile from the ocean. I've raised my children here, and they have enjoyed the same magical childhood I was fortunate to have. My daily walks include an early morning stroll on the boardwalk, and I won't deny I love it. I love seeing the ocean every day, whether it's stormy and wintery or in the bright summer sunshine. It's a part of me—a sentiment most locals would attest to.

I have been writing about food in New Jersey on my blog, JerseyBites.com, since 2007. Doing so has afforded me the opportunity to meet passionate food lovers, farmers, fishermen, and restaurateurs. I'm excited to share some of their stories and recipes here.

Some of the restaurants you will read about have been serving Jersey Shore visitors for decades. Some are family-owned businesses with multiple generations working under one roof. Some are relative newcomers giving their all to serve innovative dishes using locally sourced produce and seafood. Most of them endured devastating damage from Hurricane Sandy, but through the help of their communities, staff, and customers, they are back and better than ever.

New Jersey has a landscape and food culture that is all our own. We host the majority of the country's boardwalks, we enjoy some of the most beautiful beaches, and we have miles and miles of fertile farmland and five commercial fishing ports. That local food is fresh and delicious, and eating it supports the state's economy. After all, when you buy local seafood, you support not only the fishing crew but the boat repairman, the dock master, and the infrastructure that keeps the region's waterways safe. This book celebrates all that is local, fresh, and Jersey.

Dining at the Jersey Shore means something different to everyone. I wanted this book to embrace all types of dining experiences, from diners to fine dining, from corner bakery to off-the-boat, sunset views, raw bar casual and everything in between. I hope you enjoy reading it, trying the recipes, and visiting the contributors who have been so generous with their time and talents in the making of this book.

11

BREAKFASTS

EGGS OSCAR

FROM

THE BUTTERED BISCUIT

YIELD:
2 SERVINGS

Eggs Oscar (shown opposite) boasts a combination of simple yet elegant flavors—tender asparagus, succulent crabmeat, and rich hollandaise. It's a Jersey spin on traditional eggs Benedict and a staple on the menu at the Buttered Biscuit. In a pinch, you can make hollandaise from a packaged mix; add fresh lemon juice and a dash of Tabasco to brighten the flavor. Another variation: serve on a biscuit instead of an English muffin.

8 asparagus stalks, ends trimmed

½ teaspoon salt

Pinch ground black pepper

1 tablespoon olive oil

1 tablespoon white vinegar

4 eggs

2 English muffins

1 pound lump crabmeat

Hollandaise sauce, either homemade or from a packet (such as Knorr brand)

1. Preheat oven to 350°F. Toss asparagus with salt, pepper, and olive oil. Arrange on a baking sheet and roast for 10 minutes, until fork-tender but not mushy.

2. Meanwhile, fill a medium saucepan halfway with water. Add vinegar and bring to a rolling boil over high heat. Crack one egg into a small bowl or ramekin and then gently slip it into the pot; repeat with remaining eggs, one at a time. Lower heat, cover, and cook for about 4 to 5 minutes. While eggs cook, toast English muffins. Use a slotted spoon to carefully remove cooked eggs and place them on a paper-towel-lined plate to drain.

3. Place 4 ounces crabmeat on each muffin half. Top with 2 asparagus stalks, 1 poached egg, and hollandaise. Serve immediately.

CREDIT: The Buttered Biscuit

THE BUTTERED BISCUIT

Husband-and-wife team David and Elizabeth McAllister have worked in the restaurant industry all their lives, and in 2011 they decided to start a place of their own. They're both big fans of breakfast foods and they wanted to create a menu and atmosphere that they could enjoy every day. When trying to decide what to call their new restaurant, they toyed with names like Elizabeth's or Babette's. But when Dave suggested "The Buttered Biscuit," Elizabeth says, "It made me feel warm and cozy, and I knew that was it."

For a front-row seat on the action, grab a stool at the counter. You'll get the chance to chat with the super-friendly staff and maybe make a few friends of your neighbors. Winner of the Taste Awards for Best Breakfast and the TripAdvisor Award of Excellence, the Buttered Biscuit has won the hearts of many locals for its fresh ingredients and innovative recipes. Don't miss the Buttered Biscuit Scramble, the biscuits and gravy, and a side order of the house-made corned beef hash. If you're going on a Sunday, get there early to avoid a wait.

15

Eggs Oscar

THE JERSEY GUY

BREAKFAST CLUB SANDWICH

FROM

BROAD STREET DINER

— YIELD: —

1 SANDWICH

Pork roll (also known as Taylor Ham) is a New Jersey specialty. It's a pork-based processed meat widely available throughout the region—but not so widely outside it. Look for it in any Jersey grocery store, near the bacon. This breakfast sandwich is a great way to try it—especially after a night out at the Shore!

3 slices pork roll (such as Trenton or Taylor brand)

3 slices white bread

2 tablespoons mayonnaise

3 slices American cheese

2 fried eggs

3 slices tomato

2 leaves green leaf lettuce

4 club-style toothpicks

1. In a large skillet over medium-high heat, cook pork roll for about a minute on each side. Toast bread and, while warm, spread with mayonnaise; top each piece of bread with a slice of cheese.

2. To assemble: Place one slice of toast on a plate and top with cooked pork roll. Place a second slice of toast on top of pork roll, followed by eggs, tomatoes, and lettuce. Top with remaining slice of toast.

3. Pierce sandwich with toothpicks and then cut into four triangles. Serve with home fries or hash browns.

CREDIT: Broad Street Diner

BROAD STREET DINER

Open year-round, seven days a week, the Broad Street Diner in Keyport is a fun part of Jersey Shore history. It resides in an original Jerry O'Mahony diner built in the 1950s and is one of only a handful of classic diners still operating in the Garden State. Ownership changed hands several times over the years; it was Stanley's Seaport Diner when current owners Nicolas and Maria Kallas purchased the restaurant in January 2015. Looking for a change in their lives, Nick and Maria fell in love with the town of Keyport and the idea of serving the bayshore community. They purchased the spot and opened the Broad Street Diner.

The couple sources as much locally grown produce as possible from farmers' markets. You can keep up with their creative, seasonal specials on their Facebook page. The diner is known for its knockout soups, including cheeseburger deluxe, split pea with Parmesan croutons, matzoh ball, and french onion.

When visiting a vintage diner, the best seat in the house is at the counter. The waitress may even call you "Hun" as she refills your coffee cup or serves you a red velvet milkshake or the popular Brunch Burger. Enjoy the trip back in time!

17

THE BRUNCHWICH: PORK ROLL

FROM

THE COMMITTED PIG

YIELD:
1 MASSIVE SANDWICH

In this inventive sweet and savory "brunchwich," a national favorite (french toast) meets a local classic (pork roll).

FRENCH TOAST

4 eggs

¼ cup heavy cream

¼ cup half-and-half

2 tablespoons ground cinnamon

¼ cup granulated sugar

1 tablespoon butter

2 thick slices challah bread

SANDWICH FILLING

5 thick slices pork roll

3 slices uncooked bacon

3 slices yellow American cheese

1 tablespoon butter

1 egg

Maple syrup, for serving (optional)

1. For the french toast: In a bowl, whisk eggs, cream, half-and-half, cinnamon, and sugar. Heat a large nonstick pan over medium heat for 1 minute. Melt butter in pan. Dip bread on both sides in egg mixture and place in pan. Cook for about 5 minutes on each side, flipping once with a spatula, until outside is golden brown and center is medium-firm to the touch. Remove from pan and cover to keep warm.

2. For the filling: In a large frying pan or griddle over medium heat, cook pork roll and bacon for about 4 minutes, flipping once. Top pork roll with cheese and cook for 1 minute more. Remove from pan and cover to keep warm.

3. Heat a small nonstick pan over low heat and melt butter. Crack egg into pan. Cook for about 2 minutes, until white is set. Flip egg with a spatula and cook for another few seconds.

4. Place one slice french toast on a plate. Top it with pork roll, then bacon, and then fried egg. Place the second piece of toast on top and serve with maple syrup (if using). Consume. And then nap.

CREDIT: Jerry Rotunno, chef/owner

THE COMMITTED PIG

When you ask chef and owner Jerry Rotunno how he came up with the name for his restaurant, his answer is quick and concise: "The best way to explain the difference between involvement and commitment is explained by the dish bacon and eggs—the chicken is involved, the pig is committed."

Evidently, pigs are not the only ones committed where Chef Rotunno's menu is concerned. The restaurant is known far and wide for its burgers, made with a hanger steak, short rib, and brisket blend supplied by North Jersey's Pat LaFrieda Meats.

Brunch is also a big deal at the Committed Pig. Such a big deal, in fact, that they serve it seven days a week. Show up when the front door opens on Saturdays and Sundays or expect a wait. Breakfast offerings include Cookie Dough Pancakes and a section on the menu dedicated to pork roll sandwiches like the "Kitchen Sinker"—with "XX-tra meat, XX-tra American cheese, fried egg, bacon, and avocado."

Located on Main Street in the quaint town of Manasquan, the Committed Pig is housed in a historic building (formerly a Masonic temple) with cool, rustic details like exposed brick walls and a tin ceiling. Open year-round, the restaurant is the perfect place to enjoy comfort food, whether in the dog days of summer or the dead of winter. Just remember to get there early.

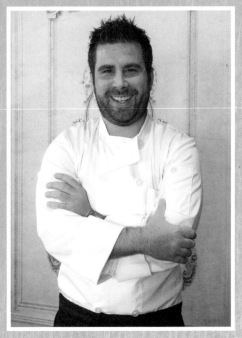

Chef/owner Jerry Rotunno

21

NORMANDY BEACH

GRILLED JERSEY PEACHES

WITH

GREEK YOGURT AND GRANOLA

FROM

LASOLAS MARKET

— YIELD: —

10 SERVINGS

Make this super-simple peachy treat after grilling dinner. Enjoy it as a sweet finish to a meal or store it overnight and serve for breakfast.

PEACHES

10 Jersey peaches, halved and pitted

3 to 4 tablespoons coconut oil (or canola oil or ghee)

Kosher salt, to taste

Dark brown sugar, to taste

GRANOLA

3 cups rolled oats

1 cup sliced almonds (or cashews)

¾ cup shredded sweetened coconut

¼ cup dark brown sugar

1 teaspoon ground cinnamon

¼ cup maple syrup

¼ cup coconut oil

¾ teaspoon salt

1 cup dried cranberries

TO SERVE

1 pint good-quality plain Greek yogurt

Powdered sugar, for dusting (optional)

Fresh mint, for garnish (optional)

1. Heat grill to high. Brush peaches with coconut oil and season with salt and brown sugar. Grill, cut side down, for about 5 to 7 minutes, or until golden brown but still slightly firm.

2. Preheat oven to 250°F. In a large bowl combine oats, almonds, coconut, brown sugar, and cinnamon. In another bowl combine maple syrup, coconut oil, and salt. Add wet ingredients to dry ingredients, stirring to combine.

3. Spread mixture onto sheet pans and bake for 1 hour, stirring every 15 to 20 minutes, until slightly browned. Stir in cranberries.

4. Arrange grilled peaches cut side up. Top each with a dollop of Greek yogurt and sprinkle with granola. Garnish as desired: dust with powdered sugar, drizzle with more maple syrup, and/or top with fresh mint.

CREDIT: Lasolas Market

LASOLAS MARKET

Lasolas Market is a seasonal market offering everything from fresh produce to prepared foods. It typically opens shortly after St. Patrick's Day and stays open until mid-October (if the weather cooperates). Established in 2002 about a mile south of its current location in Normandy Beach, the market was relocated in 2012. Ten days after the end of the new location's first season, Hurricane Sandy struck. With eighteen inches of water throughout the building, Lasolas was back to square one. "That first season after Sandy was rough all around," says Lasola's Josh Gryvatz. "But we (and the surrounding towns) have been steadily fighting our way back."

The market is now back to its old self. It features freshly baked bread from New York (show up at 7 a.m. and score it still warm from the oven). And it stocks fresh New Jersey produce, which also is featured in salads and prepared dishes.

Lasolas (*las olas* means "waves" in Spanish) is a family affair. The Gryvatzes, owners of Double D Market and Catering in Old Bridge, have been in the food business for nearly thirty years. When the opportunity arose to open a second location "down the shore," they jumped at the chance. Mom Berta and son Jonathan run the weekly operations, with help on weekends from father George and sons Jeremy and Josh.

Lasolas's team of hardworking servers and cooks keeps the market moving during the busy season. Their lunch rush, which can last four to five hours, offers no time for breaks. Loyal customers know they might have to wait for their food, but it'll be worth it.

Lasolas Market chef and operations manager Josh Gryvatz

23

BLUEBERRY SCONES

FROM

MUELLER'S BAKERY

YIELD:
12 SCONES

One of the most exciting times in New Jersey is blueberry season, which usually lasts from early July through early August. Many local farms offer pick-your-own, so supply is always close at hand. These scones (see photo, opposite) showcase the beauty beyond the shore.

3½ cups bread flour

⅓ cup granulated sugar

5 tablespoons (⅓ cup) butter, softened

3 teaspoons baking powder

Pinch salt

4 fluid ounces buttermilk

4 fluid ounces heavy cream

1 large egg

1 tablespoon vanilla extract

2 cups fresh or frozen blueberries

1. Preheat oven to 350°F. In the bowl of an electric stand mixer fitted with the paddle attachment, combine flour, sugar, butter, baking powder, and salt. Mix briefly on low speed to distribute evenly.

2. In a bowl, whisk together buttermilk, cream, egg, and vanilla extract. Turn the mixer on low speed and slowly pour wet mixture into dry ingredients. Increase speed to medium and mix for 1 to 2 minutes, until dough softens. Return to low speed and mix in blueberries until combined. Try not to over-mix or dough will turn blue.

3. With an ice cream scoop, drop dough onto parchment-paper-lined baking sheets; you should have 12 scones. Bake for 25 to 35 minutes (if berries are fresh, about 25 minutes; longer if berries are frozen). When done, scones should be light brown and firm to the touch. Serve warm or cool.

CREDIT: Mueller's Bakery

MUELLER'S BAKERY

Open from Valentine's Day through December 31, Mueller's Bakery—tucked away in the small, storybook town of Bay Head—is known for its famous crumb cakes and other sinfully satisfying baked treats. It's a local tradition to stop by early, pick up something for breakfast, and take it to the beach for a great start to a beautiful summer day.

When Mueller's was devastated by Hurricane Sandy—the store had more than four and a half feet of water throughout—many feared it would be the end of the local institution. The bakery's reopening, just in time for Memorial Day Weekend 2013, was a hopeful sign the community needed to see. Although there was still no phone service and they could accept cash only, the iconic bakery opened its doors to show everyone it would be back.

Mueller's uses about one ton of blueberries during the summer season, featuring them in pies, scones, muffins, shortcakes, flans, tortes, cheesecakes, and much more. It's their customers' favorite fruit. But the crumb cake is Mueller's signature dish, baked daily and shipped worldwide.

Mueller's was established in the early 1950s, but its location had served as a bakery since at least 1897. Just think about all the bakers who have worked in this spot over the past hundred-plus years!

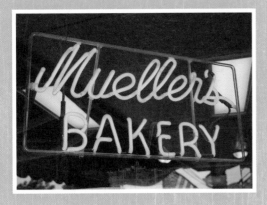

Blueberry scones

25

JERSEY CAKES

FROM

THE CHICKEN OR THE EGG

YIELD:
8 PANCAKES

The Chicken or the Egg owners Mark and Craig Cohen originally named this recipe Shaunie Cakes, after Mark's wife, Shaunie, which is ironic because she was a vegetarian at the time. Then it hit them: One of the main ingredients, pork roll, is a New Jersey standard. So they changed the name to Jersey Cakes. Whatever they're called, these hotcakes are sweet, salty, and delicious.

4 strips cherrywood-smoked bacon (or any good-quality bacon)

4 thin slices pork roll, Taylor brand preferred

2 links breakfast sausage

2 large eggs

1 pint buttermilk

¼ cup vegetable oil

1 tablespoon granulated sugar

½ teaspoon salt

2 cups all-purpose flour

1 teaspoon baking soda

Scant 1 tablespoon baking powder

Butter, for cooking and serving

Maple syrup, for serving

1. In a large frying pan or griddle over medium-high heat, cook bacon, pork roll, and sausage until bacon is crisp, sausage is browned, and pork roll is slightly crisp. Remove from heat and set aside.

2. In a large bowl, combine eggs, buttermilk, and oil. In another bowl combine sugar, salt, flour, baking soda, and baking powder. Add dry ingredients to wet and mix by hand (not with an electric mixer). A few lumps are okay. Transfer to a pitcher or gravy boat.

3. Heat a griddle (preferred) or nonstick frying pan over medium heat. Melt a little butter in the pan (unless using nonstick pan). While pan is heating, dice bacon, pork roll, and sausage into small pieces.

4. When pan is hot, pour batter into 3-inch-diameter circles and immediately sprinkle each with some of the meat mixture. When bubbles begin to form (after about 2 to 3 minutes), flip pancakes with a spatula and cook for another 2 minutes or so, until golden brown. Serve topped with butter and syrup.

CREDIT: The Chicken or the Egg Restaurant

THE CHICKEN OR THE EGG

Late one night back in 1991, Mark and Craig Cohen were sitting around craving really good wings but had nowhere to get them. A few weeks later, what began as a late-night craving hatched into a career: The Chicken or the Egg was born.

Many people wonder where the name of their restaurant came from. When the guys first opened (in a rented space that had been a breakfast eatery), money was tight. So the pair decided to operate as a breakfast-only restaurant until they could afford to buy fryers (for those wings) and update the kitchen. They decided on a name that would embrace both eggs and chicken. Hence, The Chicken or the Egg, which would eventually become known to regulars by the affectionate nickname CHEGG.

The wings that inspired the endeavor have garnered several awards over the years, including Best Wings in New Jersey, South Jersey, and Jersey Shore honors from *New Jersey Monthly*, *South Jersey Magazine*, *Islander Magazine Readers Choice*, and *Philadelphia* magazine—multiple times. CHEGG was first runner-up at the prestigious LBI Chowderfest cookoff for their New England and Manhattan clam chowders. The restaurant has also won Best Breakfast Islander Reader's Choice and honorable mention for breakfast several times over the years.

Locals know to arrive early because the wait can be long. Those truly in the know use the restaurant's wait-list app No Wait, which lets patrons add their party from home, the road, or wherever they're enjoying Long Beach Island.

Despite the fame the Chicken or the Egg has developed over the years—a visit from *Man vs. Food*'s Adam Richmond in 2010 was a boon—the restaurant sticks to its simple philosophy of serving good food at fair prices. That's kept the crowds coming for twenty-four years and counting.

Owner Mark Cohen

STARTERS AND SIDES

ALLAGASH STEAMERS

FROM

MARIE NICOLE'S

YIELD:

2 SERVINGS

Clams may be available year-round in New Jersey, but they're undeniably associated with summers at the shore—especially when steamed with fresh herbs and beer. For this recipe (shown opposite), choose the freshest littlenecks that have tightly closed shells or snap closed when you tap them. A few slices of crisp grilled bread for dipping in the flavorful broth and you're done!

2 pounds littleneck clams

4 tablespoons cornmeal

1 tablespoon olive oil

1 tablespoon sliced shallots

1 tablespoon chopped garlic

1 tablespoon grated orange zest

1 cup Allagash White beer

¼ cup fresh orange juice

3 tablespoons cold butter

1 tablespoon chopped fresh parsley

1 tablespoon chopped fresh oregano

½ teaspoon kosher salt

1. Clean clams by covering them, along with cornmeal, with water for 10 minutes. Rinse, being sure to wash off all cornmeal.

2. In a saucepan over medium-high heat, warm olive oil for 1 minute. Add shallots, garlic, and orange zest and cook for 90 seconds. Add beer, orange juice, and clams. Cook, covered, for 4 to 5 minutes. Discard any unopened clams.

3. Add butter, herbs, and salt. Let stand for 1 minute, until butter is melted. Transfer to a bowl and serve. Enjoy!

CREDIT: *Marie Nicole's*

32

MARIE NICOLE'S

Since its 2000 inception, Marie Nicole's (named after restaurateur Jim Barnabei's mother) has received multiple awards, including *Wine Spectator*'s Award of Excellence for offering an array of wines from many regions at different price points. The restaurant has also won Best of the Shore from both *Philadelphia* magazine and *South Jersey Magazine* as well as OpenTable's Diners' Choice Award. But it's their famous stuffed lobster tail that has become an island favorite.

Chef August Zimmerman prides himself on his close relationships with local farmers and food purveyors. Keeping up on trends and growing seasons helps him showcase "Jersey Fresh" ingredients. The restaurant even grows its own herbs in a garden out back.

Dining is available inside and out during warm weather. (On Fridays during high season, arrive early to snag a much-coveted seat at the bar.) Try the signature cocktail, the Marie Nicole—a combination of Grey Goose La Poire, a few secret ingredients, and fresh ginger purée, served icy cold in a martini glass and garnished with an orange twist. Or sample the local favorite, a cucumber gin and tonic mixed with freshly made cucumber purée.

While you're dining, be sure to look for the picture of the original Marie Nicole. It hangs above the window at the bar, watching over everything with a big smile.

Allagash steamers

33

JUMBO LUMP CRAB CAKES

WITH

CHILI REMOULADE AND JERSEY TOMATOES

FROM

CHEF MIKE'S ABG

— YIELD: —
10 5-OUNCE CRAB CAKES

This colorful and flavorful appetizer (shown opposite)—a customer favorite at Chef Mike's ABG—makes great party food.

CRAB CAKES
1 small red bell pepper, diced

1 small green bell pepper, diced

1 small yellow bell pepper, diced

1 small scallion, sliced

3 eggs

1 cup panko bread crumbs

¼ cup mayonnaise

3 tablespoons Dijon mustard

2 teaspoons granulated garlic

1 teaspoon black pepper

1 teaspoon kosher salt

3 pounds jumbo lump crabmeat, drained completely

Blended oil, for cooking

CHILI REMOULADE
1 cup mayonnaise

½ cup relish

½ cup ketchup

5 tablespoons Tabasco sauce

¼ cup fresh lemon juice

3 tablespoons Cajun seasoning

TO SERVE
2 pints Jersey cherry tomatoes, halved

Microgreens, for garnish

1. For the crab cakes: In a mixing bowl, combine all ingredients except crab. When mixed, slowly fold in crab, trying not to break up the lumps. When well mixed, form into 10 patties.

2. In a pan over medium heat, add a small amount of oil, just enough to coat the bottom of the pan. Pan-fry crab patties until golden brown, about 5 minutes. Flip and cook until golden brown, about 5 minutes more. Remove from pan.

3. For the chili remoulade: Place all ingredients in a mixing bowl and stir to combine.

4. To serve: Place a few tomatoes on each plate, top with a crab cake, drizzle with remoulade, and garnish with microgreens.

CREDIT: Chef Mike's ABG

CHEF MIKE'S ABG

Some chefs take refuge behind closed kitchen doors, but Mike Jurusz is a man about town. If he isn't competing in a local food event, he's judging one. Winner of the Best Jersey Shore Burger Contest two years in a row, the Boss of the Sauce in 2013, and many more, Jurusz likes a good challenge.

In 2013, he was up for the challenge when he purchased what was then the Atlantic Bar and Grill and renamed it Chef Mike's ABG (short for Atlantic Bar and Grill). The restaurant is perched high on the dunes with a bird's-eye view of the Atlantic Ocean—every seat is the best seat in the house. Diners can also enjoy a view into the kitchen, and locals are known to poke their heads in to ask what the specials are for the night.

If it's your first time to the restaurant, you may be a little confused when your GPS puts you on the doorstep of the Island Beach Motor Lodge, but do not be dismayed. Just follow the long parking lot toward the ocean and Chef Mike's ABG will be waiting for you. The building was built in the 1950s using concrete to withstand storms. Even Hurricane Sandy had no effect on this rock-solid structure.

The menu in the summer is created around what's in season in New Jersey. It includes raw bar offerings, tapas, and an extensive turf menu for those who shy away from the surf side. The restaurant also has a lively bar scene. One of the most popular drinks is the Bloody Mary. According to Chef Mike, "I wanted it to be a meal and not just a drink, and it started the whole movement on the Jersey Shore for outrageous bloodies."

Jumbo Lump Crab Cakes

35

CAPE MAY

BRIE EN CROÛTE

FROM

THE MAD BATTER RESTAURANT

YIELD:
8 SERVINGS

This festive appetizer or brunch entree is outstanding when served with fresh berries and grapes. It pairs well with many wines—in fact, the Mad Batter Restaurant often serves this version at its special wine dinners.

1 egg

1 sheet store-bought frozen puff pastry, thawed at room temperature for about 30 minutes

½ cup apricot or raspberry preserves

⅓ cup dried cranberries, soaked in warm water until softened

¼ cup toasted sliced almonds or walnuts

1 13.2-ounce round brie

1. Line a baking sheet with parchment paper and spray with nonstick cooking spray. Preheat oven to 400°F. Whisk together egg and 1 tablespoon water; set aside.

2. Place thawed pastry on a lightly floured surface. Unfold and roll sheet into a 14-inch square. With a paring knife, trim corners to form a circle; if desired, save trimmed dough to decorate after assembly. Spread preserves over pastry, leaving a 1-inch border. Sprinkle cranberries and almonds over preserves. Top with brie.

3. Brush border of pastry with egg mixture. Fold two opposite sides of pastry over the cheese. Trim unfolded sides to 2 inches from edge of cheese and then fold those onto cheese. Press edges of dough to seal. Place seam side down on the prepared baking sheet. Decorate top with pastry scraps if desired. Brush top of dough with egg mixture.

4. Bake for 20 minutes, or until golden brown. Serve warm.

CREDIT: The Mad Batter Restaurant at the Carroll Villa Hotel

THE MAD BATTER RESTAURANT

The Mad Batter is one of the most beloved restaurants in Cape May. Family-run for thirty-nine years, it is credited with starting the dining renaissance in this Victorian seashore resort. Chefs Lisa Erdly and Robert Barto serve customer favorites like eggs Benedict, their award-winning pancakes, blackened fish sandwiches, and crab cakes to between 800 and 1,000 people per day during the summer.

Open year-round for breakfast, lunch, and dinner, the restaurant insists on Jersey-grown fresh vegetables and fruit when in season. Its tomato and mozzarella salad is a summer staple, and you'll find local asparagus accompanying most of the entrees. Local scallops fresh off the boat are often featured, and local berries star in the dessert fruit bowls.

According to the locals, you want to get there early for breakfast, especially on Sundays. And if you want a seat at the bar for happy hour, show up by 3 p.m. While you're there, try the Mad Batter Bloody Mary or a mimosa made with freshly squeezed orange juice. For dinner, ask about the daily fresh fish special.

The Mad Batter is located in the Carroll Villa Hotel, which was constructed in 1882 as a seaside escape for families. Built in the Italian villa style of architecture, the hotel features a cupola affording a panoramic view of Cape May. The building has been lovingly restored, maintaining its Victorian charm while bringing it into the twenty-first century with energy-saving and environmentally friendly updates, including solar panels. If you're lucky enough to score a seat on the front porch, you'll have a lovely view of historic Jackson Street with its Victorian buildings and passing horse-drawn carriages.

Over the years, the Mad Batter has won numerous awards, including Best Brunch, Best Happy Hour, and Best Breakfast from Capemay.com.

37

CAJUN SHRIMP AND GRITS

FROM

BRICKWALL TAVERN AND DINING ROOM

YIELD:
4 APPETIZER SERVINGS

One of the longest-running dishes at Brickwall, this comforting pairing of Cajun-spiced seared shrimp and creamy, cheesy grits is my personal favorite dish on the menu.

1 cup Quaker Quick 5-Minute Grits

½ cup grated Parmesan cheese, or to taste

16 large shrimp (sold as "U15" size), peeled and deveined

5¾ teaspoons Cajun Seasoning (see below)

Canola oil, for searing

1. In a large pot over high heat, bring 4 cups water to a boil. Stir in grits, cover, and reduce heat to low. Cook for 5 to 7 minutes, stirring occasionally. Stir in cheese.

2. In a bowl, toss shrimp with Cajun seasoning to coat.

3. In a skillet over medium to high heat, warm a scant amount of canola oil. Add shrimp and sear on one side, about 3 minutes. Turn shrimp, sear for 3 more minutes, cover, and remove pan from heat. Let stand for 2 to 3 minutes to finish cooking shrimp.

4. Divide grits among four plates, arrange 4 shrimp on top of each, and serve.

CAJUN SEASONING
YIELD: SCANT 2 TABLESPOONS

1 teaspoon paprika

1 teaspoon smoked paprika

¾ teaspoon dried thyme

¾ teaspoon dried oregano

¾ teaspoon garlic powder

¼ teaspoon salt

¼ teaspoon ground black pepper

1 teaspoon cayenne pepper

Combine all ingredients. Store leftover seasoning blend in an airtight container at room temperature.

CREDIT: Brickwall Tavern

BRICKWALL TAVERN AND DINING ROOM

When it opened in 2006, Brickwall Tavern and Dining Room on Cookman Avenue in Asbury was one of the first restaurants to ignite the restaurant renaissance in this infamous Jersey Shore town. It is the oldest of several restaurants owned and operated by the Smith Group (known as Smith), and it has remained the same funky, cozy, totally casual spot since its inception.

Brickwall's long bar, with twenty-four beers on tap, greets you as you enter. With its comfort-food menu (think meatloaf and roast turkey with all the fixins) and constantly rotating selection of craft beers, this is the perfect place to hang out and relax. In addition to the regular offerings of burgers, sandwiches, and irresistible pub fare like tater tots, fried brussels sprouts, pierogies, and deviled eggs, Brickwall posts daily lunch and dinner specials on its Facebook page (don't miss the "beer float of the day," a featured adults-only ice cream soda). Smith has designed Brickwall's concept to speak to the blue-collar ethic and the simplicity of a job well done. Exposed pipes, industrial lighting, and brick walls make for a stylish yet laid-back atmosphere.

41

One of the most popular appetizers at Fratello's, these oysters are locally sourced from the Long Island Sound. "Even though we have delicious Italian food," Chef Gerardo Martinez explains, "it's always great to find a unique dish that sets us apart from the other seafood restaurants at the Jersey Shore." Use the freshest oysters you can find, preferably locally sourced.

OYSTERS GRATINÉE

FROM

FRATELLO'S RESTAURANT

YIELD:
4 SERVINGS OF 6 OYSTERS EACH

2 tablespoons (¼ cup) butter, melted

3 cups coarse panko bread crumbs

Pinch chopped fresh rosemary

1 teaspoon chopped tarragon

1 tablespoon chopped Italian parsley

½ cup shredded Parmesan cheese

1 tablespoon crushed black pepper

24 Blue Point Long Island Sound oysters

1 cup kosher sea salt

½ cup pickling spice

8 wedges lemon

SAUCE

1 cup (2 sticks) butter

¼ cup lemon juice

1. Preheat oven to 375°F. In a large mixing bowl, use your hands to mix melted butter, panko, rosemary, tarragon, parsley, Parmesan, and black pepper until well combined.

2. Carefully shuck oysters: Use a kitchen towel or glove to hold an oyster firmly in one hand. Insert the tip of an oyster knife into the hinge, using gentle pressure and turning the oyster until the knife goes into the shell. Twist the knife to pop open the shell. Use the blade to sever oyster from top shell; discard top shell. Leaving the oyster and its juice in the bottom shell, slip the blade under oyster and sever it from the bottom shell. Repeat with remaining oysters.

43

3. Place 1 teaspoon bread crumb mixture on top of each oyster. Place oysters on a baking sheet and bake for 12 minutes, or until golden brown. While they bake, make a bed of ¼ cup kosher salt on each of 4 plates.

4. Remove oysters from oven and immediately transfer to the prepared plates, 6 oysters per plate. They will be very hot coming out of the oven. Transferring them immediately allows the oysters to take on the flavor of the coarse salt. Garnish with pickling spice and 2 lemon wedges per plate.

5. Make the sauce. In a saucepan over medium heat combine butter and lemon juice and cook until butter melts. Drizzle over oysters.

CREDIT: Chef Gerardo "Paco" Martinez, Fratello's Restaurant

FRATELLO'S RESTAURANT

Fratello's is a charming local restaurant (think *Cheers* sans Rhea Perlman) in picturesque Sea Girt, New Jersey, offering an early dinner menu, live music on Thursday and Friday nights, and a warm and friendly atmosphere year-round.

The menu has something for everyone, from Italian classics to an impressive seafood selection to some of the best steaks in the area. One of the more popular starters is the artichoke hearts française, and the flounder française entree is a favorite. For something totally different, try the Shrimp on Angels: jumbo shrimp wrapped in prosciutto and angel hair pasta, broiled, and served with horseradish sauce. All of Fratello's pasta dishes can be made gluten-free.

For the best seat in the house, request one of the first two booths on the left, where you get a bird's-eye view of all the action from a comfortable, private setting. Or grab a seat under the green-and-white striped awning on the street overlooking the park. The bar is also an extremely popular place to dine; try one of the special martinis, which Fratello's claims are the biggest in town. Among the fifteen choices available are the Fratello-tini—champagne, Stoli Ohranj, Chambord raspberry liqueur, a splash of prosecco, and sour mix—and the Italian Surfer, featuring Malibu coconut rum, amaretto, pineapple juice, and a splash of freshly squeezed orange juice.

SOUPS AND SALADS

SEA ISLE CITY

CREAMY CRAB SOUP

FROM

MARIE'S SEAFOOD

YIELD:
4 SERVINGS

This easy, filling soup is based on a customer favorite at Marie's. It's good any time of year, but especially in the coldest part of winter, when you need a taste of summer to remind you of the shore.

¼ cup salted butter

1 cup diced onions

1 cup diced celery

⅓ cup all-purpose flour

1 quart half-and-half

¼ cup cooking sherry

1 pound jumbo lump crabmeat

1 tablespoon chopped fresh parsley

Salt, to taste

Ground black pepper, to taste

1. In a 3-quart saucepan over medium heat, melt butter. Add onions and celery and cook, stirring, for 5 minutes, or until softened. Add flour and whisk until blended.

2. Slowly add half-and-half, whisking constantly. Bring to a boil and then lower heat. Simmer, whisking occasionally, for 20 minutes.

3. Add sherry, crabmeat, and parsley and continue to simmer for 10 minutes.

4. Season with salt and pepper and serve.

CREDIT: Marie's Seafood

MARIE'S SEAFOOD

On Forty-third and Park Road, in Sea Isle City's historic Fish Alley, stands one of the area's institutions: Marie's Seafood. Maria and Joseph Misiano emigrated from Italy in 1909 and settled in Brooklyn, New York, where they waited for their three daughters to join them. In 1916, the whole family moved to Sea Isle City—as did many immigrants from Ponza, Italy—because it reminded them of the waterways they had left behind in their homeland.

In 1949, the family opened a small fish market in the popular fishing community. Three generations later, it has grown into one of the most popular dining destinations in the area. It features classic Italian dishes that showcase locally caught seafood, such as lobster fra diavolo over linguini and soft-shell crabs served with spaghetti.

Today the restaurant is led by grandson Butch and great-grandson Steve, who also manages the fish market. You can get fresh raw fish to take home and prepare or cooked seafood either for take-out or to eat on their deck overlooking the water. Marie's Seafood is a BYOB and offers local wines along with its signature dishes.

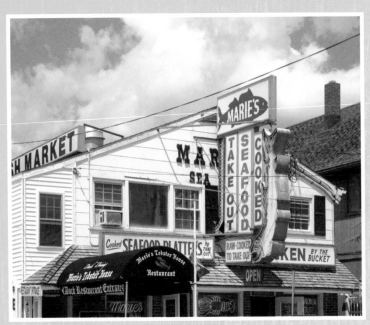

49

A FISHERMANS
PRAYER
LORD GIVE ME GRACE
TO CATCH A FISH SO
BIG THAT EVEN I, WHEN
TELLING OF IT
AFTERWARDS MAY
NEVER NEED
TO LIE.

"Sixty years of chef experience—along with fresh, local ingredients—go into every batch of our New England clam chowder," says Shrimp Box co-owner George Gyftakis. This make-at-home version is creamy, hearty comfort food at its best.

NEW ENGLAND CLAM CHOWDER

FROM

THE SHRIMP BOX

YIELD:
8 CUPS

4 tablespoons salted butter

⅜ cup all-purpose flour

2 tablespoons olive oil

1 cup diced onions

1 cup diced celery

5 ¾ cups clam broth or home-made clam stock

2 cups chopped fresh clams with juice

3 cups diced Idaho potatoes

1 cup heavy cream

1 cup half-and-half

1 teaspoon chopped fresh parsley

1 to 1½ teaspoons salt, or to taste

Ground black pepper, to taste

1. Make a roux: In a medium saucepan over medium heat, melt butter. Add flour and cook, whisking constantly, for 2 to 5 minutes. Set aside to cool.

2. In a large pot over medium heat, heat olive oil. Add onions and celery and sauté for a few minutes, until onions are translucent and vegetables are soft. Add clam broth. Simmer uncovered over medium heat for 30 minutes.

3. Add clams, with their liquid, and potatoes to broth. Bring to boil, lower heat, and simmer uncovered for 30 minutes.

4. Add some soup liquid to roux, a ladle at a time, to soften it. Stir roux into soup. Bring to a boil over medium heat, and then simmer uncovered for 1 minute.

5. Add heavy cream, half-and-half, and parsley. Heat through, letting soup simmer. Season with salt and pepper. Serve.

CREDIT: The Shrimp Box and Outside the Box Patio Bar

51

52

THE SHRIMP BOX

In 1940, the land where the current Shrimp Box now sits was purchased to become a commercial fishing dock. The restaurant began as a small take-out stand, but after several years it was moved inside to the retail fish market and its seating was expanded.

The restaurant's growth has been supported by a devout local following cultivated under the current ownership of the Gyftakis family, who remodeled the property and built a harborside patio. Today, the Shrimp Box is a local institution. On any given day you can see regulars stopping by to bring party leftovers for the staff or asking the employees about their latest family news.

If you're seated outside, look for the hand-painted stones that locals decorate to use as paperweights for the checks. You can't beat a patio seat during sunset—the whole town comes out, so arrive about forty-five minutes ahead to secure a table.

If you've got a big appetite, try the Captain's Platter—a sampler of broiled lobster tail, scallops, shrimp, salmon, stuffed shrimp, flounder Florentine, clam casino, and oyster Rockefeller. The Creamsicle Crush and the Orange Crush cocktails, both made with orange juice squeezed to order, scream summertime.

Voted Best Seafood Restaurant in Ocean County by *Asbury Park Press* and Best of the Jersey Shore: Favorite Restaurant by NJ.com, the Shrimp Box is a must for any visit to Point Pleasant Beach.

53

Langosta owner Marilyn Schlossbach explains: "When I was growing up at the Jersey Shore, my dad had a wonderful tomato garden that flourished every summer. Whenever I make this soup, the aromas immediately bring me back to the days I would spend with my father harvesting vibrant, fresh, ripe tomatoes and sweet basil." Serve this soup hot or cold, along with garlic croutons or toasted French bread.

ROASTED TOMATO AND BASIL SOUP

FROM

LANGOSTA LOUNGE

YIELD:
6 TO 8 SERVINGS

2 pounds ripe heirloom or Jersey tomatoes, halved lengthwise

¼ cup good-quality olive oil, plus 2 tablespoons for sautéing

1 teaspoon sea salt

½ teaspoon freshly ground black pepper

1 cup chopped sweet yellow onions (about 1½ Vidalia or Maui onions)

3 garlic cloves, minced

4 garlic cloves, roasted

2 tablespoons unsalted butter

¼ teaspoon crushed red pepper flakes

1 16-ounce can good-quality plum tomatoes with their juice

1 cup fresh basil leaves, packed

2 cups vegetable or chicken stock

1 teaspoon granulated sugar

1. Preheat oven to 400°F. In a large bowl, toss fresh tomatoes, ¼ cup olive oil, salt, and pepper with a wooden spoon. Spread in a single layer on a baking sheet and roast for 45 minutes.

2. In an 8-quart stockpot over medium heat, warm 2 tablespoons olive oil. Add onions, minced and roasted garlic, butter, and red pepper and sauté for 10 minutes, until onions start to brown.

55

3. Add canned tomatoes, basil, and stock to stockpot. Add sugar and oven-roasted tomatoes, including the liquid on the baking sheet. Bring to a boil and simmer, uncovered, over low heat for 40 minutes.

4. Transfer mixture to a blender and puree. Taste, adjust seasonings, and serve.

CREDIT: Marilyn Schlossbach, Langosta Lounge

LANGOSTA LOUNGE

Since 2009, Asbury's Langosta Lounge has been serving up "vacation-inspired" fare on the Asbury Park boardwalk. That vacation could be to Thailand, Tijuana, or anywhere in between. Year-round you can count on a fun and adventurous meal for lunch and dinner seven days a week. Langosta's relaxed vibe makes it an Asbury Park favorite, whether you're stopping by at the funky bar (try the Langostarita) or meeting up with friends for a casual dinner, inside or out.

One of the menu's biggest crowd pleasers is the Maui Monkey Bread for Life, a Hawaiian sweet bread that is served in a savory grilled pineapple butter and sprinkled with island sea salt. One hundred percent of the proceeds from the dish goes to the employees' healthcare fund.

Owner Marilyn Schlossbach also owns Pops Garage, which has locations in Asbury and Shrewsbury, as well as the cozy Labrador Lounge, her flagship restaurant in Normandy Beach. Schlossbach is known for her many local philanthropic activities, including an annual free Thanksgiving dinner in Asbury Park for those in need.

Owner Marilyn Schlossbach

57

SPICED CORN CHOWDER

FROM

REMINGTON'S

YIELD:
ABOUT 8 CUPS

Sweet Jersey corn is the star of this chowder, which also features spicy, smoky pork. Use the leftover corn stock as a base for other meals: crab boil, clam boil, lobster boil, risotto, corn pudding, cornbread, pasta broth, cornbread stuffing, and more.

8 ounces thick-cut bacon, diced ¼ inch

8 ounces yellow onions (about 1 medium-sized onion), diced ¼ inch

½ cup all-purpose flour

8 cups Corn Stock (see page 59), hot

Reserved corn kernels from stock recipe (see page 59)

1½ pounds gold potatoes, ½-inch dice

1 pint heavy cream

¼ ounce fresh thyme (about 10 sprigs), tied together with butcher twine

1 to 4 fresh bay leaves (depending on size)

1½ tablespoons kosher salt

½ tablespoon fresh, finely ground black pepper, or to taste

½ teaspoon Tabasco sauce, or to taste

½ tablespoon Worcestershire sauce

A few fresh chives, sliced small

4 ounces smoky, spicy chorizo, such as Palacios Chorizo Picante, skinned and chopped (optional; find it at gourmet food stores or online)

1. In a heavy-bottomed pot over medium heat, cook bacon slowly until fat is rendered and bacon is on the verge of crispy. Add onions and cook for about 10 minutes more, until translucent.

2. Dust mixture with flour and stir to combine well. Cook for 2 more minutes, stirring constantly with a spoon. Make sure there are no lumps!

3. Slowly add hot corn stock 1 cup at a time, whisking constantly. No lumps! Add corn kernels, potatoes, cream, thyme, and bay leaves. Turn heat to low and cook uncovered for 30 minutes, stirring every few minutes to prevent potatoes and corn from sticking and burning.

4. Add salt, pepper, Tabasco, and Worcestershire sauce. Remove and discard thyme bundle and bay leaves. Taste and correct seasoning as necessary. If you'd prefer a sweeter soup, add wildflower honey or light agave nectar a little at a time to taste. (The black pepper and Tabasco can be lessened for a less spicy soup.)

5. Serve hot and garnish with fresh chives and chorizo pieces.

CORN STOCK
YIELD: ABOUT 16 CUPS

10 ears fresh Jersey sweet corn, in husks

1 to 4 fresh bay leaves

½ ounce fresh thyme

1 teaspoon black peppercorns

1. Shuck corn cobs, reserving silk and husks. With a sharp knife, cut kernels from cobs; reserve kernels for chowder recipe (see step 3 above).

2. In a large pot, combine cobs, silk, husks, bay leaves, thyme, peppercorns, and 2 gallons water and bring to a boil over high heat. Lower heat and simmer uncovered for at least 1 hour (ideally 2 to 4 hours). The stock should reduce by about half.

3. Strain stock through a fine-mesh sieve or coffee filter; discard solids. Store leftover stock in the freezer. (Use it in vegetable-based dishes, combined with other vegetables or meats for richer stocks, risotto, corn pudding, cornbread, tea, pasta broth, etc.)

CREDIT: Remington's

REMINGTON'S

Open year-round on Main Street in Manasquan, Remington's is an elegant yet casual restaurant founded in 2010 that serves a seasonal menu.

Regulars will tell you to try the signature cocktail, a Basil Lemon Drop Martini, developed by Remington's beloved bartender Kristin Trainor, who has been with the restaurant since the beginning. Away from the bar, you'll find several spots to take in the comings and goings of Main Street pedestrians, and a seat by the fish tank offers a bird's-eye view of the bustling kitchen. Couples can find a romantic spot near the fireplace, and big families will be comfortable at one of the large tables in the main dining room.

Owners Rod Kerr and Matthew Schmidt are longtime friends—one is a Culinary Institute of America graduate, the other has a family history in hospitality—who saw a Craigslist ad for a restaurant that was for sale. They decided to take the plunge. Deciding on the establishment's name was not as easy. After vetting about a hundred options, they landed on the winner by way of Schmidt's pet green-winged macaw, Remington. If you look closely, you will see a feather in the restaurant's logo, an homage to their feathered friend.

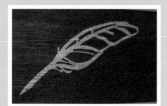

61

CHILLED ROASTED NEW JERSEY SWEET CORN AND BUTTERMILK SOUP

FROM

LOUISA'S CAFÉ

YIELD:
6 SERVINGS

"In the summer, we receive beautiful New Jersey sweet corn, along with peppers, onions, and parsley, from Beach Plum Farm, which is just down the road," says Louisa's Café's co-owner, Honna Riccio. "This refreshing soup is a customer favorite on hot summer nights. We love the browned golden kernels of fresh roasted corn."

2 red bell peppers, or any sweet variety

Kernels from 6 ears Jersey sweet corn

2 large sweet onions, sliced into 1-inch-thick rings

¼ cup plus 2 tablespoons olive oil

1½ quarts buttermilk

½ cup packed chopped flat-leaf parsley leaves, plus more for garnish

1 tablespoon kosher salt

1 teaspoon ground black pepper

1. Place peppers directly on top of a gas flame and roast until soft and charred, about 5 minutes on each side. With tongs, remove from heat and place in a glass bowl. Cover with foil and let steam for 15 minutes. Once cool, remove stems, seeds, and skins, and chop.

2. In a large cast-iron skillet over high heat, cook corn. Stir after a couple of minutes and cook for another 4 to 5 minutes, until golden brown and just tender. Let cool.

3. Drizzle onions with 2 tablespoons oil. Place on a hot grill and cook for 5 to 7 minutes per side, until tender and beginning to caramelize. Let cool, remove charred skin, and chop.

4. In a food processor or with an immersion blender, puree half the corn and onions with buttermilk and ¼ cup olive oil. Stir in remaining corn and onions, parsley, roasted peppers, salt, and black pepper. Adjust seasoning. Refrigerate, covered, for at least 2 hours. Serve cold with freshly chopped parsley.

CREDIT: *Honna Riccio, Louisa's Café*

LOUISA'S CAFÉ

The original owners of Louisa's Café's, Louisa and Doug Hull, established the restaurant in 1980. It was one of the original "farm-to-table" restaurants in New Jersey. When the couple was ready to retire in 2014, former employee Will Riccio stepped up to carry on the tradition. He and his sister Honna are Cape May natives who worked at the restaurant during their teenage years.

The pair now run the restaurant using the same local focus they learned from Doug and Louisa. They work directly with Beach Plum Farm, which is less than two miles away. The menu changes daily according to what is available from the farm. (Check the chalkboard.)

The little building was moved to its current location in the late 1800s. The mystery, though, is where it came from. In the late 1700s, Cape May was home to numerous small taverns catering to shore visitors. Most were destroyed in a fire in 1878, but historians believe some survived on the periphery of town. They're known as the "lost taverns of Cape May" because they were moved or subsumed into buildings constructed around them. The size of the café's building—and some of the details found during renovation— lead us to believe that Louisa's is one of the lost taverns of the 1780s.

Louisa's is open from Memorial Day to Labor Day (except Mondays) starting at 5 p.m. In the off-season the restaurant opens Friday to Sunday, except in January, when it's closed.

Owners Will and Honna Riccio

63

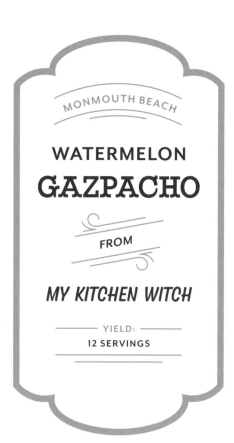

WATERMELON GAZPACHO

FROM

MY KITCHEN WITCH

YIELD:
12 SERVINGS

"I love summer fruits and vegetables, and I love soup!" says My Kitchen Witch owner Karyn Jarmer. "But in the summer it's just too hot to cook, so I tried blending watermelon with some of my favorite vegetables and came up with this awesome soup." This recipe involves no cooking and very little mess.

2 fennel bulbs, roughly chopped

4 garlic cloves

2 red peppers

2 yellow peppers

2 jalapeño peppers

½ watermelon, cubed (about 10 cups cubed)

1 64-ounce can tomato juice

1 cup lemon juice

1 cup olive oil

Salt, to taste

Ground black pepper, to taste

1. In a food processor, pulse fennel, garlic, peppers, and jalapeños until mixture is slightly chunky; do not over-pulse. Pour into a large bowl.

2. Add watermelon, tomato juice, lemon juice, olive oil, salt, and pepper. Stir. Cover and refrigerate until chilled. Serve cold.

CREDIT: My Kitchen Witch

MY KITCHEN WITCH

When chef/owner Karyn Jarmer ran a catering business in Manhattan, one of her clients was *The Rosie O'Donnell Show*. On the day Madonna was scheduled to be a guest, the show called at the last minute to ask for breakfast instead of lunch. That gave Jarmer about thirty minutes to improvise. She pulled it off, earning the nickname "Kitchen Witch." It stuck.

Monmouth Beach is known for its spooky old Victorian houses, and My Kitchen Witch also has its fair share of witches. Jarmer's employees are affectionately referred to as "the witches," and the theme runs through the menu items—including Eggs Benewitch and, of course, an ample selection of "sandwitches."

Jarmer loves to shop locally. The café's signature drink is the organic Ozmopolitan; fresh-squeezed lemonade with berries. Regulars will tell you to get there before opening (8 a.m.) on weekends to avoid a wait, and on Saturdays you can usually expect some over-the-top steak and eggs for breakfast, thanks to prime rib Friday nights. While you savor the smells from the kitchen and wait for your meal, see how many witchy objects you can spy throughout this quirky café.

65

CAPE MAY

BEACH PLUM FARM SALAD

FROM

THE EBBITT ROOM

YIELD:
4 SERVINGS

Fresh strawberries are one of the first signs that summer is right around the corner. Combining them with peppery radishes, bitter lettuces, and nutty cheese—as in this salad—enhances their sweet, juicy flavor.

VINAIGRETTE

½ cup champagne vinegar

1 tablespoon Dijon mustard

3 tablespoons honey

1½ cups grapeseed oil

Chopped fresh herbs (such as tarragon, thyme, rosemary, chives, and/or parsley), to taste

Salt, to taste

Freshly ground black pepper, to taste

SALAD

4 cups summer lettuces, such as Muir, New Red Fire, Helvius, or Red Magenta

1 cup fresh strawberries, sliced

½ cup radishes shaved on a mandoline slicer

½ cup manchego cheese sliced with a vegetable peeler

¼ cup toasted sunflower seeds

1. Make the vinaigrette: In a blender, combine vinegar, mustard, and honey on medium speed. With blender running, pour in grapeseed oil in a slow, steady stream until mixture forms a uniform emulsion. Transfer to a bowl or container and whisk in chopped herbs. Season with salt and pepper.

2. In a large mixing bowl, combine lettuces, strawberries, radishes, cheese, and sunflower seeds. Season with salt and pepper.

3. Lightly drizzle with about ½ cup of the vinaigrette and toss gently, using salad forks or tongs. Transfer to a large plate or bowl and serve immediately. Store any leftover vinaigrette in an airtight container in the refrigerator.

CREDIT: The Ebbit Room/Chef Matt Crist

THE EBBITT ROOM

The Ebbitt Room resides in the Virginia Hotel, a beautifully restored 1879 landmark building in Cape May's historic district. Established in 1989, this sophisticated yet casual restaurant takes farm-to-table dining very seriously—so much so, they bought the farm. The Beach Plum Farm in West Cape May, that is. In addition to glorious local produce, Beach Plum also offers pork, chicken and duck eggs, turkeys, and a wide variety of flowers and herbs. What the farm can't provide, chef Matthew Crist sources locally, including oysters, scallops, tuna, and flounder.

An insider tip: try the Beach Plum Farm Berkshire pork rib chop. It's straight off the farm and has become the most popular dish on the menu. The most romantic seat in the house? Table 12, a private spot in the corner, hidden behind the bar. If you're more the social type, plant yourself on the front porch, where you can grab a cocktail and some appetizers and watch the beachgoers heading home. Ask for some popcorn!

Of course, you'll need something to wash down that popcorn. The Ebbitt Room incorporates local herbs from Beach Plum to create their seasonal cocktails. The old-fashioned is popular, and a little Beach Plum birdie told us that the margaritas are a must.

Called "superb" and "memorable" by the *New York Times* and the recipient of many awards, including the 2014 OpenTable Diners' Choice Award, the Ebbitt Room is a Cape May experience not to be missed.

Chef Matthew Crist

67

THE DIVING HORSE TOMATO SALAD

FROM

THE DIVING HORSE

YIELD:
4 SERVINGS

High-quality Jersey tomatoes are available only in the summer, when they're flavorful and abundant. The Diving Horse likes to take advantage of them while they last. They're a touchstone of a New Jersey summer, and this salad (shown opposite) is a great way to enjoy them.

½ cup ricotta cheese

1 pint heirloom cherry tomatoes

1 teaspoon sherry vinegar

1 tablespoon olive oil

1 shallot, diced small

1 tablespoon chopped chives

2 tablespoons basil oil

Salt, to taste

Ground black pepper, to taste

1. With an electric mixer on high speed, whip ricotta until smooth. Just before serving, halve tomatoes. In a stainless-steel bowl, toss them with sherry vinegar and olive oil.

2. Add shallots and chives. Transfer ricotta to a serving bowl and top with tomatoes. Season with basil oil, salt, and pepper and serve.

CREDIT: The Diving Horse

THE DIVING HORSE

Restaurateur Dan Clark, a South Jersey native who spent many a summer with his family in Avalon, now owns a summer shore home of his own. Naturally, he wanted to find a way to spend more time there. As co-owner of Philadelphia's popular restaurants Pub & Kitchen and Fitler Dining Room, Clark came up with the perfect solution: open a restaurant in Avalon.

The restaurant is named after Atlantic City's famous Diving Horse, which used to plunge into a 60-foot tank with a young woman riding on its back. The menu features new American fare highlighting coastal ingredients, many sourced from nearby farms and Cape May County fishermen. Menu items change almost daily. Ask the locals and they'll tell you to order the soft-shell crabs whenever you can.

The restaurant features a modern farmhouse interior with reclaimed fixtures and bright, oversized windows. The patio, which is enclosed by tall, lush landscaping, holds three large picnic tables for communal seating and a private eight-seat round table, often used for chef's tasting dinners, all beneath strands of vintage Edison-bulb string lights. If you're looking for the best seat, ask for table 21, which has a great view of Avalon Circle in the heart of town.

This inventive BYOB is open only for the season (from May to mid-September), so dive in while you can.

The Diving Horse Tomato Salad

CHARRED JERSEY TOMATO SALAD

WITH

SWEET CORN, ASPARAGUS TIPS, AND HERB YOGURT

FROM

IRON ROOM RESTAURANT

— YIELD: —
5–6 SERVINGS

This is the perfect dish to accompany any summer dinner. It's fresh, healthy, and—best of all—full of local New Jersey ingredients. You can char the tomatoes in a hot pan, but for best results use an outdoor grill. After all, it is summer!

3 ears Jersey sweet corn

1 bunch Jersey asparagus

3 to 4 tablespoons extra-virgin olive oil, divided

5 to 6 large Jersey beefsteak tomatoes, quartered

Salt and pepper, to taste

1 pint good-quality Greek yogurt

1 bunch scallions, roughly chopped

½ bunch oregano, roughly chopped

Juice of 2 lemons

1. With a sharp knife, cut corn kernels off cobs. Chop off the top third of each asparagus stalk; you want only the tips. Reserve remaining asparagus for another use.

2. In a medium saucepan over medium to high heat, warm 1 tablespoon of the olive oil. Sauté corn and asparagus for about 3 to 5 minutes, or until lightly cooked but still crisp. Do not overcook. Let cool. (This can be done an hour or so before serving.)

3. Preheat an outdoor grill. Toss tomatoes with salt, pepper, and 2 to 3 tablespoons of the olive oil (just enough to coat them). Place tomatoes on the hottest part of the grill and heat until one side is charred. Immediately toss tomatoes with corn mixture.

4. In a mixing bowl, stir together yogurt, scallions, oregano, lemon juice, and salt and pepper to taste.

5. Serve this salad family-style, with the yogurt sauce alongside, so that guests can dress their salads. Or plate individual portions, with a dollop of yogurt sauce on each.

CREDIT: Kevin W. Cronin

70

IRON ROOM RESTAURANT

Despite its tiny footprint and off-the-beaten-path location, the Iron Room has won many awards in its short lifespan. Zagat named it one of the ten hottest restaurants on the Jersey Shore. It was also named Best American Restaurant in Southern NJ, Best New Restaurant in Southern NJ, and Critic's Pick for Best Bar Scene by *New Jersey Monthly*. *Atlantic City Weekly* called it the "ironclad innovator," and *South Jersey Magazine* awarded it Best Small Plates in its annual Best of South Jersey list. The wine program has won a two-glass award from *Wine Spectator* magazine.

The Iron Room is known for chef Kevin Cronin's inventive dishes, including Asian BBQ hanger steak with sweet and sour brussels sprouts, udon mac and cheese, and steak tartare.

The best seat in the house is probably at the chef's table. There, parties of five or more can enjoy an interactive experience in which the chef visits the table and tailors the meal to guests' requests. If you're more interested in the bar scene, stop by on a Friday night. The kitchen stays open until 2 a.m., and rumor has it that guests can sample small bites, like a croquette or deviled egg.

The Iron Room's signature cocktail is the Iron Root, a potent potable made of New Holland wheat whiskey with root liqueur, maple syrup, Coca-Cola, and cherries. It tastes just like a grown-up root beer.

Chef Kevin Cronin

71

Served chilled, this refreshing salad epitomizes summertime with the freshest ingredients available. Make it just for yourself or mix up a larger batch to share with friends and family.

LONG BRANCH

DUNGENESS CRAB SALAD

WITH

LEMON VINAIGRETTE

FROM

AVENUE

YIELD:
1 SERVING

2½ ounces chopped romaine hearts (about 1⅔ cups)

1½ tablespoons Lemon Vinaigrette (see page 74), divided

Salt, to taste

Freshly ground black pepper, to taste

2½ ounces Dungeness crab meat

1 tablespoon diced heirloom baby tomatoes

1 tablespoon chopped seedless cucumber

2 tablespoons chopped avocado

1 teaspoon thinly sliced chives

1 teaspoon chopped Italian parsley

2 leaves romaine hearts, for garnish

Sprinkle coarsely ground black pepper, to finish

1. In a small mixing bowl, toss chopped romaine with ½ tablespoon of the vinaigrette; season with salt and pepper. Place romaine on the bottom of a serving bowl.

2. In a mixing bowl, combine crab, tomato, cucumber, avocado, chives, and parsley. Season with remaining vinaigrette, adjusting salt and pepper if necessary. Place mixture on top of chopped romaine.

3. Insert romaine leaves between the bowl and salad, like rabbit ears. Finish with a sprinkle of black pepper and serve immediately.

73

LEMON VINAIGRETTE
YIELD: ABOUT 4 CUPS

⅔ cup freshly squeezed lemon juice

⅓ cup plus 4 teaspoons sweet wine
vinegar (such as Banyuls)

3 cups extra-virgin olive oil

Salt, to taste

Ground black pepper, to taste

In a medium bowl, combine lemon juice and vinegar. Slowly pour in oil and mix all ingredients with a high-speed immersion blender. Season to your liking with salt and pepper. Refrigerate in a plastic container for up to 10 days.

CREDIT: *Dominique Filoni, Avenue Restaurant*

74

AVENUE

When the most popular dish on an oceanside restaurant's menu is boeuf bourguignon, you know you're in for a special meal. Established in 2006 and designed by renowned London-based architect David Collins, Avenue is a modern blend of the Parisian brasserie and the luxurious beaches of St. Tropez.

Thierry Carrier, Avenue's general manager and director of operations, was born in St. Julien, France. Carrier is a third-generation hospitality professional educated at the prestigious Lycée Hôtelier Savoie Léman in Thonon-les-Bains. He worked in Geneva, London, South Beach, the Hamptons, and New York City before landing in Long Branch, New Jersey, to help conceive and run Avenue.

At the age of sixteen, chef Dominique Filoni graduated with honors from the intensive culinary program at the Lycée Hôtelier Institute in Hyères, France. In 2003, Filoni was inducted into the Maîtres Cuisiniers de France, making him the youngest French master chef in the United States at that time. In 2004, he was named one of America's best new chefs by *Food & Wine* magazine.

During the summer, the best seat in the house is on the terrace overlooking the ocean; during the winter, try cozying up in front of the fireplace to enjoy views of the Atlantic. Avenue's glorious bar is the focal point of the dining room; the floor-to-ceiling bottles lining the wall behind the bar are backlit at night to stunning effect. Head upstairs to the third floor for dancing, or venture outside to the beach bar for some salty air and a cool cocktail. No matter where you settle, you'll be surrounded by breathtaking ocean views.

Few things are more beautiful than a perfectly dressed tuna, with its skin in shiny blue, black, gray, and sometimes flashes of vibrant yellow, nestled in ice. Inside this formalwear is a red so immaculate, it needs only to be enhanced by a minimalistic approach.

GRILLED TUNA NIÇOISE SALAD

WITH

DIJON-THYME VINAIGRETTE

FROM

BLACK-EYED SUSANS

YIELD:
4 SERVINGS

VINAIGRETTE

1 teaspoon Dijon mustard

¼ cup lemon juice

1 cup good-quality olive oil

2 tablespoons minced shallots

2 tablespoons picked fresh thyme leaves

Salt, to taste

Ground black pepper, to taste

SALAD

2 tablespoons salt, plus more to taste

½ pound haricots verts

16 medium fingerling potatoes

6 sprigs fresh thyme, divided

1 lemon

12 cherry tomatoes (a variety works best)

1 cup good-quality olive oil, plus more for rubbing tuna

Ground black pepper, to taste

4 (6-ounce, 2-inch-thick) pieces #2 grade or better yellowfin or bigeye tuna

½ cup boquerones (vinegar-and-oil-marinated anchovies)

1 cup niçoise olives, pitted and coarsely chopped

4 hard-boiled organic eggs, peeled and halved

1 bunch watercress

1. Make the vinaigrette: In a small bowl, mix mustard, lemon juice, and olive oil. Add shallots, thyme leaves, salt, and pepper. Set aside.

2. In a pot over high heat, bring 2 quarts water to a boil. Prepare a bowl of ice water. Add 2 tablespoons salt to pot. Blanch haricots verts, uncovered, for about 30 seconds, until al dente. Transfer immediately to ice water to stop the cooking.

77

3. Slice lemon in thirds. In a large pot, combine sliced lemon with potatoes, 3 thyme sprigs, and salt to taste. Cover with cold water, set over high heat, and bring to a simmer. Cook until potatoes are fork-tender. Drain and let cool. Slice potatoes lengthwise and set aside. Discard other solids.

4. Preheat oven to 400°F. Toss tomatoes with the remaining thyme sprigs, olive oil, salt, and pepper. Arrange on an ovenproof baking dish and bake for about 10 minutes, until just blistered and softening. Remove from oven and chill immediately.

5. Season tuna with salt and pepper and rub with olive oil. Grill over high heat, about 1 minute on each side, until medium rare. You want to sear the tuna well without overcooking it. Remove from heat and let rest for 20 seconds. Cut grilled tuna on a bias into thirds.

6. In a medium bowl, combine potatoes and boquerones and dress with 2 tablespoons vinaigrette. In a separate bowl, combine haricots verts and olives.

7. On a serving platter, arrange haricots verts, alternating with potatoes and tomatoes. Place tuna and eggs alongside vegetables. Drizzle with vinaigrette. Garnish with watercress and serve.

CREDIT: Christopher Sanchez

BLACK-EYED SUSANS

Open April through October, Black-Eyed Susans is not just a local favorite but a restaurant customers travel great distances to visit. Voted Zagat Top 10 in NJ in 2015 and a *New Jersey Monthly* Critic's Pick for New American and Seafood in 2012 and 2014, the BYOB is known for its innovative dishes, raw bar, and fabulous desserts.

Executive chef Christopher Sanchez and his wife, Ashley Pellegrino, were lifelong summer residents of Harvey Cedars before starting Black-Eyed Susans, so they have always been familiar with the 105-year-old building that eventually became home to their restaurant. Throughout its history, the building has been a post office, a general store, and a market, among other things.

Sanchez and Pellegrino are dedicated to sourcing everything they can locally. Sanchez makes the trip to Viking Village seafood market five days a week to collect the freshest fish possible. Produce comes from New Jersey local farm distributor Zone 7 and neighboring farms, along with whatever the couple manages to grow in their garden. Regulars will tell you the best time to dine is at 5 p.m., when the restaurant is peaceful and you'll get your choice of the best seats in the house.

Black-Eyed Susans bakes sourdough and other fresh breads on the premises to supply the restaurant, for take-out, and for sale weekly at the Surf City farmers' market.

Executive chef Christopher Sanchez

79

JERSEY PEACH, HEIRLOOM TOMATO, AND LOBSTER SALAD

WITH

PEACH DRESSING

FROM

AMA RISTORANTE AT DRIFTWOOD

YIELD:
6 APPETIZER SERVINGS

"This recipe [shown opposite] is one of my favorites," says Ama executive chef Charles Lesbirel. "Even though it features Maine lobster, it's all about New Jersey produce. When you use such high-quality ingredients like Jersey peaches and tomatoes, you don't want to do too much to the dish so that the ingredients' flavors shine through."

DRESSING

2 medium-size ripe Jersey peaches, pitted

4 tablespoons white balsamic vinegar

1 tablespoon local honey

½ cup extra-virgin olive oil

Pinch kosher salt

SALAD

3 medium Jersey heirloom tomatoes, diced into large cubes (try to find an assortment of red, yellow, and green; it really brightens up the salad!)

½ pound cleaned, cooked Maine lobster meat, cut into large chunks

2 medium-size ripe Jersey peaches, pitted and diced into large cubes

½ seedless cucumber, sliced paper-thin

5 to 6 fresh basil leaves

2 pinches kosher salt

Pinch freshly ground black pepper

1. Make the dressing: In a blender, combine peaches, vinegar, and honey and blend on medium speed until smooth. Turn blender to low speed and slowly drizzle in olive oil. Add salt.

2. In a mixing bowl, combine tomatoes, lobster, diced peaches, cucumbers, and basil. Lightly mix in about ½ cup peach dressing (less or more for your liking), salt, and black pepper. Place in small salad bowls and serve. Store any leftover dressing, covered, in the refrigerator for up to 2 days.

CREDIT: Chef Charles Lesbirel, Ama Ristorante

AMA RISTORANTE AT DRIFTWOOD

Ama (the Latin word for *love*) opened in 2012 on the second level of Driftwood Cabana Club. Dining at the restaurant is fantastic year-round, but locals recommend the many midweek specials offered from September to June. During summer, a prix fixe menu is served daily for dinner and all day Sunday.

Executive chef Charles Lesbirel is an avid hunter, fisherman, and gardener. He understands that the closer a chef is to his sources, the better the flavor of his food. The most popular dish is Misto di Terra—a daily seasonal vegetable antipasto featuring gorgeous Jersey vegetables.

Ama has been racking up the awards since opening its doors. These include TripAdvisor's Award of Excellence for 2013, 2014, and 2015; NJ Monthly's New & Notable for 2013; OpenTable's Diners' Choice for 2014 and 2015; and *Wine Spectator*'s 2015 Award of Excellence.

Left: Jersey Peach, Heirloom Tomato, and Lobster Salad;
right: Executive chef Charles Lesbirel

81

WATERMELON, SPINACH, AND BRANDIED PECAN SALAD

FROM

WAYPOINT 622

YIELD:
5 SERVINGS

The ingredients in this summer salad (shown opposite) can be easily prepared ahead of time—toss everything together right before you serve it. Feel free to throw in a few blueberries for the 4th of July. With the watermelon and Gorgonzola, it will be a fun patriotic dish! This simple salad also works well with baby arugula substituted for the spinach.

4 tablespoons butter

1 cup pecans

2 fluid ounces brandy

1 cup light brown sugar

½ cup apple cider vinegar

½ cup sherry

1 ½ cups olive oil

Juice of 1 lime

½ cup strawberry jelly

Salt, to taste

Ground black pepper, to taste

1 tablespoon honey

¼ cup julienned mint

1 1-pound bag baby spinach

1 ½ cups cubed watermelon

3 ounces Gorgonzola cheese, crumbled (about ¾ cup)

¼ cup julienned red onion

1. In a 1-quart sauté pan over medium-high heat, melt butter. Add pecans, brandy, and brown sugar and cook, stirring constantly, for about 1 minute, until pecans are toasted. Transfer pan to a cooling rack.

2. Make the dressing: In a blender, combine vinegar, sherry, oil, lime juice, jelly, salt, pepper, honey, and mint and blend on high speed until emulsified.

3. In a large serving bowl, combine spinach, watermelon, cheese, onions, and pecans. Toss gently. Dress before serving.

CREDIT: Waypoint 622

WAYPOINT 622

When Union Landing, a local institution in Brielle, was purchased from the Schmidt family in 2014, the new owners began looking for a name that was maritime yet didn't label the restaurant as strictly a seafood or nautical destination. *Waypoint* is a captain's term for destination latitude and longitude; the numbers in the name come from the restaurant's street address, 622 Green Avenue.

Chef Daniel Palsi's menu features fresh American cuisine. It stars fresh seafood, of course—you can even bring in your catch to be cooked. But this year-round eatery also aims to take advantage of what every season has to offer and changes the menu accordingly.

Opened in spring 2015, the restaurant quickly moved into the busy summer season with a new private wine room and raised deck with teak wood and a marble-topped bar. It's a fun place with a Floridian feel that you don't have to leave town to enjoy. If you're looking to snag one of the coveted seats of the house, you have two choices: a table with a view of the marina or the chef's table in the catering kitchen, where you can interact one-on-one with the chef.

The locals will tell you to try the Colossal Lump Crab Cakes. For a refreshing Jersey beverage, order the Garden State Blueberry Lemonade, spectacular on a beautiful shore day overlooking the marina.

Watermelon, Spinach, and Brandied Pecan Salad

83

MAIN COURSES

JERSEY COAST GRILLED BLUEFISH

FROM

BAHRS LANDING

YIELD:
4 SERVINGS

New Jersey bluefish is a local favorite. Once caught, it should be stored at no colder than 36°F, preferably in an ice brine. Buy this fish fresh and handle it carefully until it gets to the grill. For bluefish greater than 8 pounds, remove the skin and some of the darker meat, which tends to be oily.

1 pound bluefish fillet, skin on and scales removed

¾ cup good-quality mayonnaise

1 to 2 large onions, cut into ¼- to ½-inch slices

½ Jersey tomato, sliced, or 6 to 8 whole garden cherry tomatoes

1 stalk celery, cubed

Freshly cracked black pepper

Any available fresh herbs (optional)

2 teaspoons fresh lemon juice, or to taste

1. Preheat grill to medium-high heat (about 350°F to 375°F). Lay fish skin side down on a large ungreased piece of aluminum foil. (The foil should be big enough to form a packet around the fish.)

2. Spread a thick layer of mayonnaise over fish; it should look like a thickly frosted cake. Layer onions, tomatoes, and then celery on top of fish. Sprinkle with pepper and herbs (if using) and drizzle with lemon juice. Fold foil lengthwise to seal in fish, folding in the ends. Leave enough space in the foil packet above fish so that steam can accumulate.

3. Place packet on preheated grill and close cover. Grill for about 15 minutes, depending on thickness of fillet. After 15 minutes, carefully open packet to check for doneness; you want the fish to be barely done. Fish is ready when it is opaque and flakes easily with a fork.

4. Remove packet from grill. Open foil wide. Without disturbing the fish too much, use a sharp knife or two-tined fork to poke several holes through both the fish and bottom of the packet.

5. With the foil still open, return to grill, close cover, and cook fish for another few minutes. Note: the juices and mayonnaise will drip through the foil onto the fire, which will smoke and impart a delicate smoked flavor to the fish.

6. Carefully, to avoid tearing the foil, slide or lift packet off the grill. Use a large spatula to gently slide fish off the foil onto a platter. (The skin will stick to the foil.) Serve and enjoy.

CREDIT: *Bahrs Landing*

BAHRS LANDING

Bahrs Landing has been a fixture on the shore of the Shrewsbury River since 1917. The building was originally a boathouse that was built after the Civil War. It was raised to its present level in the 1960s.

This right-off-the-sand casual restaurant is a popular destination after a long day spent on the beaches of Sea Bright and Sandy Hook or an afternoon on the boat. Visitors can relax and take in the amazing 180-degree view of the river, Sandy Hook, and the Atlantic Ocean. There's even a dockside tiki bar featuring the restaurant's signature cocktail, the Bahr-a-Cuda.

Bahrs sources local ingredients at community farmers' markets as well as from fishing boats that pull right up to their docks. Perhaps that's why the biggest crowd-pleaser on the menu, according to insiders, is the seafood sampler. Crabcake lovers, take note: Bahrs Landing's crabcake won Monmouth Park's Annual Jersey Shore Crabcake Cookoff every year from 2011 to 2014.

If seafood isn't your thing, not to worry: Bahrs offers serious German fare including Wiener schnitzel, knockwurst and bratwurst, and traditional sauerbraten. They also serve fresh-baked buttermilk biscuits and a coleslaw that's a local favorite.

89

At Quahog's, chefs Lucas Manteca and Carlos Barroz love to find sustainable fish that is under-appreciated, surprising their customers with unexpected flavors and presentation. That's why this recipe is called Trash Cakes: they use the bluefish that is so underrated, no fisherman wants it. The Fancy Slaw gets its name from the pride and effort they put into making it—it may take some time to prepare all the ingredients, but the effort is well worth it!

TRASH CAKES

AND

FANCY SLAW

FROM

QUAHOG'S SEAFOOD SHACK

— YIELD: —
4 TO 5 SERVINGS

1 pound fillet locally caught bluefish, skin on

Salt and black pepper, to taste

Juice of 4 lemons, divided

Zest of 2 oranges

¼ cup olive oil

1 green apple, peeled, diced, and kept in water mixed with a little lemon juice

1 fennel bulb, thinly diced

1 bunch scallions, chopped

½ tablespoon minced garlic

1 tablespoon local honey

1 cup sour cream

2 egg yolks, whisked

1 bunch dill, chopped

4 cups panko bread crumbs

Fancy Slaw, for serving (see page 92)

1. Soak 2 cups apple wood chips overnight. Season bluefish on the flesh side with salt, pepper, juice of 2 lemons, and orange zest. Wrap fish in plastic wrap and foil and refrigerate for 24 hours to remove some of its moisture.

2. Smoke fish in either a smoker or a hotel pan with a perforated insert. Place wood chips on the bottom pan and light chips with a torch. Place fish in the perforated pan, along with a drizzle of olive oil. Place perforated pan over bottom pan, cover pans with aluminum foil, and let fish smoke for about 1 hour, checking on the embers once in a while. After an hour, fish should be fully cooked and flaking. Refrigerate fish until ready to use.

91

3. With a fork, gently flake fish into lumps (but don't shred it). Place pieces in a large bowl and add apple, fennel, scallions, garlic, honey, the remaining ¼ cup lemon juice, sour cream, egg yolks, and dill. Carefully mix with your hands until combined; don't overmix into a paste. Refrigerate for 1 hour.

4. In a shallow dish, spread a layer of panko. Using a large ice cream scoop, form fish mixture into 4 to 5 cakes and place on bread crumbs. Dust cakes with more bread crumbs and press gently to adhere crumbs. Refrigerate cakes until ready to bake.

5. Preheat oven to 350°F. Drizzle a baking pan with a little olive oil. Place fish cakes on pan and drizzle cakes with a little more oil. Bake for 10 minutes, until golden.

6. Place a cake on each plate, top with fancy slaw, and serve.

FANCY SLAW
YIELD: 4 TO 5 SERVINGS

2 celery roots, peeled and julienned

1 bunch green kale, washed, stems removed, and cut into chiffonade

4 young carrots, julienned

2 tablespoons whole grain mustard

1 teaspoon local honey

1 teaspoon apple cider vinegar

½ cup sour cream

¼ cup mayonnaise

1 bunch chives, minced

Salt and black pepper, to taste

In a glass or stainless-steel bowl, combine slaw ingredients. Let sit for 1 hour before serving.

CREDIT: Lucas Manteca, Quahog's Seafood Shack

QUAHOG'S SEAFOOD SHACK

Quahog's Seafood Shack offers seafood with a South American twist in little Stone Harbor. Chefs Lucas Manteca and Carlos Barroz know their exotic fish. Selections like Pacu fish ribs, a South American dish that Guy Fieri swooned over when he visited for an episode of *Diners, Drive-ins, and Dives,* and Moqueca Mixta, a Brazilian seafood stew, share the menu with locally sourced seafood and plenty of fresh Jersey produce.

Established in 2008, Quahog's (pronounced "co-HOGS") was inspired by the chefs' Argentinian roots and influenced by the area—as well as the building, which, Manteca declares, "is truly a shack." That's what makes it such a fun experience: phenomenal food with a casual vibe.

For something light and refreshing, order the tuna watermelon ceviche: sushi-grade tuna, watermelon, red onion, cherry bell radish, cilantro, avocado, and ponzu sauce. Quahog's works with Windy Acres Farm in Cape May Court House, which grows vegetables for the restaurant.

The covered garden out back is a favorite place to relax over a meal. Just remember to bring the libations; Quahog's is a BYOB.

93

Umami is the subtle, delicious savory quality known as the fifth element of taste, along with sweet, salty, sour, and bitter. This dish creates umami feeling with its combination of kombu broth and dashi butter.

VIKING VILLAGE SWORDFISH

WITH

PURPLE STICKY RICE, MAITAKE MUSHROOMS, AND MUSHROOM KOMBU DASHI

FROM

THE ARLINGTON

YIELD:
4 SERVINGS

4 8-ounce portions swordfish, skin and bloodline removed

Salt, to taste

Ground black pepper, to taste

Blended oil, for cooking

4 cups cooked Purple Sticky Rice (recipe below)

4 cups Mushroom Kombu Dashi (recipe below)

2 cups maitake mushrooms, pulled apart

4 pats Dashi Butter (recipe below)

1 8-ounce package enoki mushrooms

½ cup smoked bonito flakes

1. Preheat a convection oven to 450°F with the fan on, or preheat a regular oven to 450°F. Season fish with salt and pepper. In an ovenproof large sauté pan over medium-high heat, heat oil until it smokes. Add fish. Sear for 3 minutes, flip, and transfer pan to oven. Cook to desired doneness (about 5 minutes for medium, depending on steak thickness).

2. While fish bakes, warm purple sticky rice in a small pot over medium heat. In another small pot over medium heat, warm mushroom kombu dashi.

3. In a medium pan over medium heat, sauté maitake mushrooms in oil. Season with salt and pepper.

4. Remove fish from oven. Top each steak with a pat of dashi butter. Return to oven for 2 minutes.

5. Spoon rice into 4 bowls. Top with maitake mushrooms and then enoki mushrooms (they will cook in the broth). Place swordfish on mushrooms. Top with bonito flakes. Pour dashi into bowls and serve.

95

PURPLE STICKY RICE
YIELD: 4 CUPS

4 cups purple sticky rice

⅓ cup salt

2 tablespoons baking soda

1 cup rice vinegar

⅓ cup granulated sugar

1. In a large bowl combine rice, salt, baking soda, and 4 cups water; stir. Refrigerate overnight.

2. Drain rice and transfer to a medium pot. Cover with 1 inch water. Cover pot, bring to a boil over high heat, and lower heat to maintain a simmer for about 20 minutes, until water is absorbed.

3. In a large bowl mix together rice vinegar and sugar, and then add purple rice. Allow hot rice to absorb the seasoning before serving as above.

MUSHROOM KOMBU DASHI
YIELD: 5 CUPS

1 to 2 4-by-10-inch pieces dried kombu (look for it in East Asian markets)

½ cup Hon Dashi bonito soup flakes (look for them in East Asian markets)

1 bunch scallions, trimmed

2 cups dried mushrooms or stemmed fresh shiitake mushrooms

½ cup mushroom soy sauce

In a large pot combine all ingredients with 10 cups filtered water. Bring to a boil and then reduce heat to low and simmer uncovered for 5 to 6 hours. Strain before serving.

DASHI BUTTER
YIELD: 1 POUND

1 pound unsalted butter

½ cup Hon Dashi bonito soup flakes

In the bowl of an electric stand mixer fitted with the paddle attachment, whip butter and soup flakes on low to medium speed until incorporated. Transfer mixture to a sheet of parchment paper and form in a rough log. Roll paper around butter to shape into a cylinder, twist ends to seal, and refrigerate until ready to use.

CREDIT: *Chef Brian Sabrese, The Arlington*

96

THE ARLINGTON

The Arlington opened in LBI in 2013, when it took over the old Bayberry Inn and quickly became a favorite place known for its inventive menu and craft beer selection. It is brothers Brian and Paul Sabarese's first restaurant together. They use a purveyor to source from local farms and look to Viking Village for fish and scallops. They also grow their own tomatoes, cucumbers, herbs, and microgreens.

The restaurant's name is a nod to Beach Arlington, the original name of Ship Bottom. The atmosphere is casual yet polished, with rustic hardwood floors, weathered Douglas fir tabletops, and Windsor chairs—not your typical beach hangout, which makes it a nice change of pace for LBI.

The Arlington is open year-round, so you can find a cozy spot in front of the Barn Room's fireplace even in the off-season. Order the popular Korean BBQ short ribs to amp up the comfort factor. The bar room gets busy during daily happy hour (come early). On tap is a wide assortment of craft beers, including local breweries Kane, Cape May, and Carton Brewing. If you're looking for a serious cocktail, try the Barrel Aged Manhattan made with Buffalo Trace bourbon, Cinzano, and Angostura bitters.

Left: Co-owner/chef Brian Sabarese

97

ISLAND TIME FISH TACOS

FROM

JON AND PATTY'S COFFEE BAR AND BISTRO

YIELD:
4 SERVINGS

"We tell our customers to expect crispy, savory, and sweet with heat" when tasting this Mexican- and tropical-inspired dish, says Jon Talese of Jon and Patty's Coffee Bar and Bistro. Try serving these tacos with calico black bean salad and sliced jalapeños.

SLAW

1 cup shredded red cabbage

1 tablespoon fresh lime juice

2 tablespoons fresh orange juice

1 teaspoon sesame oil

¼ teaspoon curry powder

¼ teaspoon ground cumin

2 tablespoons coconut milk

1 teaspoon minced fresh ginger

Salt, to taste

Ground black pepper, to taste

DRESSING

1 teaspoon grated fresh ginger

6 tablespoons orange juice

4 tablespoons light soy sauce

2 tablespoons sesame oil

2 teaspoons honey

SALSA

1 cup chopped fresh mango

¼ cup chopped red and green peppers

¼ cup chopped tomatoes

1 tablespoon minced jalapeños

2 tablespoons chopped cilantro

2 tablespoons honey

FISH

Vegetable oil, for frying fish

4 6-ounce pieces beer-battered cod

4 small flour tortillas

Butter, for crisping tortillas

1. In a large bowl, stir together all slaw ingredients. Set aside.

2. In a small bowl, stir together all dressing ingredients. Season to taste with salt and pepper. Set aside.

3. In a medium bowl, combine all salsa ingredients, with salt and pepper to taste, and stir. Set aside.

4. In a large pot with a thermometer clipped to the side, heat oil to 375°F. Gently drop fish into oil and deep-fry for 4 to 5 minutes, until crisp and golden. Transfer to paper towels. Let cool for 1 minute and then cut into 1-inch slices. Set aside.

5. Crisp the tortillas: In a sauté pan, heat butter over medium-high heat. One at a time, place each tortilla in pan for a few seconds, until crisp and brown on one side.

6. Assemble tacos: Spoon slaw into taco shells, followed by fish, salsa, and a drizzle of dressing. Sprinkle with salt and pepper. Serve.

CREDIT: Jon and Patty's Coffee Bar and Bistro

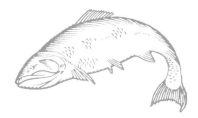

serving Dinner
Mon-Sat
5-9
The "Juice"
The Snappy Ginge
TRY ONE OF OUR
COFFE DRI

JON AND PATTY'S COFFEE BAR AND BISTRO

Jon and Patty Talese grew up in the restaurant business, met in the restaurant business, and fulfilled a lifelong dream when they opened Jon & Patty's Coffee Bar and Bistro in 2008. The couple's four children all work in the family-run restaurant. Chef Lainie Sampson is part of the family, too, according to Jon. "Chef Lainie has a big heart, is a great teacher, and runs a tight ship in the kitchen."

Located in a beautiful building dating from the early 1900s, Jon & Patty's offers plenty of outside seating under its eye-catching red awning. The restaurant has been the subject of several paintings over the years, a few of which are on display inside.

Jon and Patty's most popular dish, the Island Time Fish Tacos (shown opposite), are truly delicious. Other popular dishes include the nutty chicken salad sandwich, served on cranberry nut bread, and the veggie bomb sandwich, offered on artisan black bread or a multigrain wrap. Locals come in for the fresh juices, including Wonder Melon, Green Goddess, and Blue Crush, which are made daily. With coffee choices like the Chunky Monkey, Snicker Doodle, Salted Caramel, and many more, you're bound to find a flavor to satisfy your cup o' joe jones at the coffee bar.

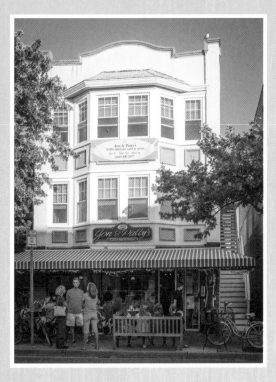

Lining the walls are a range of awards—Best of the Shore from *South Jersey Magazine*, Best Salad from the *Ocean City Sentinel*, and multiple TripAdvisor Excellence Awards. It's no wonder that Jon and Patty's continues to be a favorite destination for both locals and tourists year after year.

PAN-SEARED NEW JERSEY
BLACK SEA BASS

WITH

WHITE PEACH, TOMATO, AND BASIL SALSA

FROM

SHORE FRESH SEAFOOD

—— YIELD: ——
4 SERVINGS

A subspecies of grouper, New Jersey black sea bass is frequently found around wrecks, reefs, piers, and rock formations along New Jersey's coastline, from early May through late November. The skin is its most distinctive feature because the fish adapts to its environment. It harbors a fishnet pattern in brown, black, gray, or even indigo. The meat is firm, white, flaky, and mild, making it an excellent candidate for light summer cuisine.

2 limes

1½ pounds Jersey white peaches, pitted and sliced (about 2 cups)

1 large Jersey tomato, peeled, seeded, and diced large (about ½ cup)

2 cloves garlic, peeled and finely chopped

Leaves from 1 large sprig fresh basil (about 20 leaves), hand torn, plus more whole leaves for garnish

1 tablespoon honey

Salt

Ground black pepper

4 4- to 6-ounce skin-on fillets New Jersey black sea bass

¼ cup all-purpose flour

½ cup extra-virgin olive oil, divided

1. Make the salsa: Juice 1 lime. In a small bowl, combine peaches, tomato, garlic, basil, lime juice, honey, ¼ teaspoon salt, and ¼ teaspoon pepper. Cover and let rest at room temperature for 1 hour.

2. Preheat oven to 350°F. Pat dry both sides of fish and lightly season with a pinch each of salt and pepper. Place flour in a wide, shallow dish. In a large sauté pan over medium to high heat, warm ¼ cup of the oil until it begins to shimmer but not

102

smoke. Dredge fish in flour, shake off excess, and place in hot pan. Sear on one side for 2 to 3 minutes, until golden brown. Gently turn fish away from your body, being mindful not to splash oil, and sear on the other side for another 2 to 3 minutes.

3. Transfer fish to a baking dish and bake to desired doneness: 7 to 9 minutes for medium, 12 to 15 minutes for well-done. Fish will turn from translucent to opaque when cooked.

4. While fish bakes, discard oil from sauté pan and return pan to high heat. Add the remaining oil, then add salsa mixture, and cook for 2 minutes.

5. To serve, place 1 fillet on each of 4 plates. Divide salsa mixture among dishes, spooning over and alongside fish. Garnish each with a basil leaf and small lime wedge.

CREDIT: Executive chef Justin Benedetti

RAW BAR
CLAMS SHRIMP

Shore Fresh
Seafood Market & Restaurant
732-899-0909
TAKE OUT • RESTAURANT • CATERING

SHORE FRESH SEAFOOD

Shore Fresh Seafood market specializes in catch-of-the-day fare, partially because it shares a building with the Fisherman's Coop. "The Coop," as it is known by locals, was founded in the 1950s and serves as one of two active fishing cooperatives in New Jersey. Some members are third- or fourth-generation commercial fishermen.

Shore Fresh's chef/owner Richard Brecka is a graduate of the Culinary Institute of America, although to look at him, you might think that he spends his hours on one of the day boats moored behind his store. Rubber boots and gloves are the uniform of choice when your walk-in refrigerator opens out to the dock. Chef Justin Benedetti, who heads up the kitchen, says that "most of our product comes off of the boats still flopping rather than off of a truck in boxes packed on ice." You can't get much fresher than that.

Shore Fresh is a casual spot with patio seating and a few inside tables. Open year-round, it's where you'll find the locals stopping in for a hot bowl of clam chowder or lobster mac and cheese on cold winter days. Summer visitors come for fresh clams and local fish. You can also get takeout—just call in your order and take it to watch the parade of boats in the Manasquan inlet.

Chef Justin Benedetti

105

PECAN-CRUSTED SALMON

FROM

DOCK'S OYSTER HOUSE

YIELD:
4 SERVINGS

This dish is particularly good in early fall, when Jersey spinach and apples are readily available and wild salmon is still being caught. It also works well with good-quality farm-raised salmon.

2 cups whole shelled pecans

3 tablespoons light brown sugar

½ teaspoon sea or kosher salt, divided

4 8-ounce salmon fillets

¼ cup plus 1 teaspoon butter, melted

2 cups sour cream

¼ cup horseradish

Freshly cracked black pepper, to taste

1 cup thinly sliced smoked bacon

4 cups whole button mushrooms, sliced thin

4 large Granny Smith apples, peeled and sliced

3 tablespoons olive oil

2 pounds fresh spinach, destemmed

1. Preheat oven to 350°F. In a food processor, place pecans, brown sugar, and ¼ teaspoon salt. Pulse until coarse. Press mixture onto fillets, drizzle with butter, and arrange on a baking tray. Bake for 15 to 20 minutes, or until just opaque.

2. Combine sour cream, horseradish, salt, and pepper in a bowl. Set aside.

3. In a large sauté pan over medium heat, sauté bacon until all fat is rendered. Add mushrooms, apples, and olive oil and sauté until tender, about 3 minutes. Add spinach and toss mixture until spinach is just wilted. Season with salt and pepper.

4. Place spinach mixture onto plates, top with salmon fillets, drizzle with horseradish sauce, and serve.

CREDIT: Dock's Oyster House

DOCK'S OYSTER HOUSE

Dock's Oyster House was opened in 1897 by great-grandfather Harry "call me Dock" Dougherty. The original location was just a short walk away from where it stands now; it was moved to its current spot, a stone's throw from the Trump Plaza, in 1922. Four generations of family operators have kept Dock's alive and thriving. Today it is an iconic stop on any Atlantic City pilgrimage.

True to its name, Dock's Oyster House continues to deliver on the freshly shucked oysters that are always its most popular dish. It is also well known for its soft-shell crabs, which arrive in early April. Traditionalists will appreciate classic offerings, such as the fried oysters, "beef and reef" filet-and-lobster-tail combo, or pan-sautéed crab cakes, that have been on the menu since the restaurant's doors first opened—though today dinners run a bit more than the original price of 75 cents.

Speaking of fresh crabs, the Dougherty family (owners of Dock's and Knife and Fork Inn, page 134) have a relationship with a fisherman in Alaska who provides the restaurants with fresh king crab several times a season. It's caught on Monday and offered in the restaurants by Thursday.

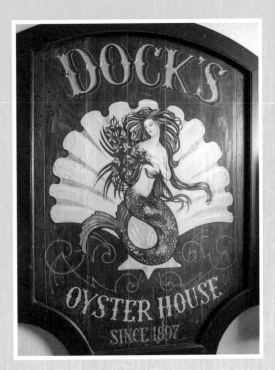

Whenever possible, Dock's incorporates local ingredients, such as tomatoes, spinach, arugula, herbs, blueberries, peaches, and asparagus. (Try the cucumber gin martini with freshly muddled cucumber!) The menu regularly changes to take advantage of what's in season.

107

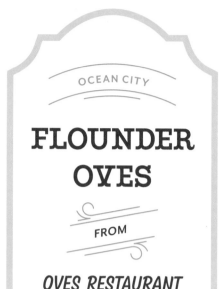

OCEAN CITY

FLOUNDER OVES

FROM

OVES RESTAURANT

YIELD:
1 SERVING

New Jersey is lucky to have an abundance of flounder, a large flatfish known for its delicate flavor and fine texture. This light dish (shown opposite) is a great way to show it off.

1 Jersey red bell pepper

¾ cup artichoke hearts

3 generous tablespoons clarified butter

1 cup all-purpose flour

1½ sides freshly caught Jersey flounder

1½ teaspoons chopped garlic

Pinch salt

Pinch white pepper

⅓ cup your favorite white wine

1 lemon wedge, plus more for garnish

Pinch chopped parsley

1. Preheat oven to 350°F. Place bell pepper directly on the top rack and roast until all skin turns black. Let cool.

2. While pepper cools, cut each artichoke heart into quarters. Scrape off all charred skin from pepper and then cut pepper from top to bottom into long strips about ½ inch wide.

3. In a saucepan set over just slightly less than the highest heat, melt butter. Spread flour on a plate. Dredge flounder in flour to coat.

4. Sauté flounder on both sides until cooked through and golden brown. (Keep the butter hot so that you sear, rather than poach, the fish.) Transfer fish to a serving plate and add garlic, artichokes, red peppers, salt, and white pepper to the hot buttered pan. Carefully pour in wine.

5. Squeeze lemon wedge into pan and allow wine to reduce for about 1 minute. Add parsley and stir.

6. Pour mixture over flounder. Garnish with a few more lemon wedges and serve. Enjoy!

CREDIT: Oves Restaurant

OVES RESTAURANT

Where do you go in Ocean City when you need to grab a beach umbrella, a bike, and some awesome crab cakes all at the same time? Oves Restaurant.

The restaurant started as a small hot dog stand in 1969, set in the middle of the sand approximately 200 yards from the boardwalk. In 1980, the boardwalk was moved closer to the stand, and the restaurant grew from there. Breakfast instantly became a hit, and ten years later dinner was added. The rest is three generations of Oves family history. It has grown from its humble beginnings to hosting a breakfast for the Ms. New Jersey Pageant. It's also garnered mentions in *Philadelphia* and *New York* magazines and even on Martha Stewart's blog. It must be doing something right.

Today, Oves is an open-air casual restaurant. Most customers like to sit right on the boardwalk, watch people walk by, and enjoy the sounds of the ocean. Those in the know book the upper deck a day or two after a full moon with the hopes of catching a glimpse of the giant orange disk rise over the ocean.

If you want to grab a meal at Oves, plan accordingly. Their season is short; typically opening the week before Memorial Day and promptly saying goodbye to the season the weekend after Labor Day.

Flounder Oves

109

Skate has a soft buttery texture and a sweet flavor similar to scallops. Ratatouille is a versatile dish that should be in every home cook's repertoire. Although this recipe dictates a traditional combination of onions, zucchini, eggplant, peppers, and herbs, feel free to experiment. And don't get too caught up in measurements—it is inherently rustic. As long as the vegetables are fresh, it will end up delicious!

NEW JERSEY SKATE

WITH

SUMMER VEGETABLE RATATOUILLE

FROM

THE BLUE PIG TAVERN

YIELD:
2 SERVINGS

2 tablespoons butter

1 tablespoon neutral cooking oil (canola, grapeseed, or vegetable)

2 skate wings, cleaned

Salt, to taste

Freshly ground black pepper, to taste

All-purpose flour for dredging

3 tablespoons olive oil

3 cups diced ripe tomatoes

1 eggplant, diced

1 yellow onion, diced

1 green zucchini, diced

1 yellow squash, diced

1 red bell pepper, diced

1 garlic clove, minced

½ to 1 cup vegetable stock

15 fresh basil leaves, torn

¼ cup chopped fresh parsley

1 tablespoon fresh thyme leaves

1. In a heavy-bottomed sauté pan large enough to fit both skate wings without crowding, heat butter and neutral oil over medium heat. Pat skate dry with paper towel and lightly season with salt and pepper. Dredge fillets in flour and shake off excess. When oil is hot, sauté fillets for about 3 minutes on each side.

2. In a large heavy-bottomed pan over high heat, warm olive oil until it just begins to smoke. Add tomatoes, eggplant, onions, zucchini, squash, and peppers and cook without stirring until vegetables brown slightly.

111

3. Add garlic and cook until fragrant. Add vegetable stock, salt, and pepper. For vegetables that are more tender, add more stock.

4. Add fresh herbs and season to taste with salt and pepper. Serve ratatouille alongside skate. Like any stew, ratatouille can be made ahead of time, refrigerated, and reheated as needed.

CREDIT: Jeremy Einhorn, executive chef, The Blue Pig Tavern

THE BLUE PIG TAVERN

The owners of the Blue Pig Tavern don't mess around when it comes to sourcing local produce. As owners of the Beach Plum Farm just about a mile from the restaurant, they grow much of the produce used at the restaurant. They also raise Berkshire pigs and smoke the meat on the property. Whether it's Berkshire bacon at breakfast, a pulled pork sandwich for lunch, or shepherd's pie for dinner, the pork at the Blue Pig is well-known.

When it's warm enough, a seat in the garden by the hedges will provide a secluded, romantic atmosphere even on a busy night. During cold months, nothing beats a seat by the fire. A local tip: the Brown Room, right next to the Blue Pig, is a great place to enjoy a drink and appetizer before dinner or an evening nightcap afterward.

The Blue Pig Tavern is part of Congress Hall, a historic hotel in Cape May. In the late 1950s, the space was made into a restaurant called the Yankee Clipper Grill. The tavern's name is derived from an upstate New York gambling troupe called the Blue Pigs, who came to Cape May in the 1840s. Some of the lighting fixtures and wrought-iron railings in the tavern were incorporated from the old Christian Admiral Hotel, located on the other side of Cape May and torn down in the 1990s.

Executive chef Jeremy Einhorn

"Tilefish has a natural fattiness that I find delicious, and its flavor is approachable by just about everyone," says Beach Tavern chef Paul Winberry. Its delicate flavor comes, in part, from the crabs and other crustaceans that make up a large part of its diet. In this dish, Winberry pairs the fish with his favorite local vegetable, sweet summer corn, for an unbeatable Jersey summer combination.

PAN-SEARED

NEW JERSEY TILEFISH

WITH

BACON CORN SUCCOTASH AND BASIL OIL

FROM

BEACH TAVERN

YIELD:
4 SERVINGS

---

4 Jersey beefsteak tomatoes

1 cup packed fresh basil

1 cup olive oil

1 1½-pound piece New Jersey–caught tilefish

4 tablespoons unsalted butter

1 cup diced uncooked bacon

1½ cups small-diced red onion

2 cloves garlic, finely chopped

3 cups Jersey sweet corn kernels, grilled

2 tablespoons finely chopped flat-leaf parsley

Salt, to taste

Ground black pepper, to taste

2 tablespoons grapeseed or other neutral oil

---

1. Fill a pot with enough water to cover tomatoes. Bring to a boil over high heat. With the tip of a paring knife, carve a small cone-shaped piece out of the stem end of each tomato and remove. Turn over tomato and use the knife to mark a small cross in the skin on the other end.

2. Prepare an ice bath. Place a few tomatoes at a time in the boiling water. When water returns to a boil, let tomatoes cook for about 1 minute longer. Use a slotted spoon to transfer them to the ice bath. Use a paring knife to peel off skins. Remove seeds and cut tomatoes into small dice. Set aside.

3. To prepare basil oil: Bring a large pot of water to a boil over high heat. Prepare a bowl of ice water. Add basil to boiling water and then immediately transfer to ice bath. Place wet

115

basil on a clean kitchen towel and wring out all the water. Place basil and olive oil in a blender and blend on high speed for 30 seconds. Note: Blending for any longer will generate excess heat, which will turn basil brown.

4. Cut fish into 4 6-ounce portions and let them sit at room temperature while you make the succotash.

5. To prepare succotash: In a large heavy skillet over medium heat, melt butter. Add bacon and cook, stirring occasionally, until bacon is crispy and fat is rendered. Add onions and stir frequently for about 5 minutes, until soft and translucent. Add garlic and cook for about 1 minute, until fragrant. Add corn, tomatoes, and parsley. Season with salt and pepper.

6. To prepare fish: Preheat oven to 350°F. In a large, heavy, ovenproof skillet, heat grapeseed oil over high heat. Season fish on both sides with salt. Place fish in skillet skin side down, pressing gently in the middle of each fillet to ensure maximum contact with the pan. Transfer skillet to the oven and bake for 2 to 4 minutes to finish cooking. Fish skin should be crispy when done.

7. Divide succotash evenly among four large plates. Place fish on top of succotash, drizzle with basil oil, and serve.

CREDIT: *Executive chef Paul Winberry, Beach Tavern*

BEACH TAVERN

The location of Beach Tavern is hard to beat. It is smack dab in the middle of Channel Club Marina in Monmouth Beach, so every seat has a view of the Shrewsbury River. The sunsets are spectacular. The high-top tables at the far end of the bar afford the best views of boats in the marina and a family of swans in spring.

Beach Tavern offers an entire dock of boat slips dedicated to day-boaters. The only way to improve upon an afternoon spent fishing, waterskiing, tubing, or cruising around the Shrewsbury and Navesink Rivers is to end with dinner here.

Chef Paul Thomas Winberry Jr. works directly with small-scale produce and protein purveyors, like Lusty Lobster of Highlands. Winberry is also a bit of a celebrity. In 2013, he competed on Bravo's *Top Chef Masters*, with former boss Douglas Keane, the chef and owner of Cyrus Restaurant in Healdsburg, California, serving as Keane's sous-chef. (They won.)

Beach Tavern lives on the former spot of Sallee Tee's Grille, a beloved local restaurant that was destroyed by Hurricane Sandy. Winberry built Beach Tavern from the ground up on the same footprint, but raised it six feet to prevent against future floods. The floors are reclaimed chestnut, an old lifeguard boat overlooks the bar, and plenty of beach-themed art is displayed throughout.

Chef Paul Winberry

117

WILDWOOD

GOLDEN TILEFISH SANDWICH

FROM

JOE'S FISH CO.

YIELD:

1 SANDWICH

Tilefish is one of chef Walter Jurusz's favorites because of its sweet buttery flavor and how easy it is to cook. This sandwich (shown opposite) is a great way to get a taste for it. You can substitute a good-quality tartar sauce or remoulade for the cilantro cream sauce, if you prefer.

CILANTRO CREAM SAUCE

1 bunch fresh cilantro

2 to 3 garlic cloves

Juice of 1 lime

2 ½ cups sour cream

2 cups mayonnaise

1 tablespoon Chef Walter J's Cuban Spice Rub (look for it in gourmet food stores around the Shore or online)

½ ounce dark rum or tequila (optional)

SANDWICH

1 4- to 5-ounce East Coast golden tilefish fillet

⅛ teaspoon Cajun blackening seasoning

1 tablespoon extra-virgin olive oil

1 brioche bun or round roll

1 lemon or lime wedge

A few leaves crisp lettuce

A few slices Jersey tomato

A few slices red onion

1. Make cilantro cream sauce: In a blender, combine all ingredients and blend on medium speed until smooth. Set aside.

2. Season both sides of fish with Cajun seasoning. In a nonstick sauté pan over medium-high heat, warm oil. Add fish and cook, uncovered, for 2 to 3 minutes. Flip and cook for another 2 to 3 minutes, or until opaque in the center. It should have a nice dark reddish-brown color. Remove from heat.

3. Spread sauce on bottom of bun, add tilefish, and squeeze lemon or lime over fish. Top with lettuce, tomato, and red onion. Serve with pickles, coleslaw, or potato salad.

CREDIT: Chef Walter J. Jurusz, Morey's Piers & Beachfront Waterparks

JOE'S FISH CO.

The ambiance at Joe's Fish Co. at Morey's Surfside Pier is unmistakably boardwalk but Joe's has been reinventing boardwalk food since 2010. Leading the charge is Culinary Institute of America graduate Walter "Wally" Jurusz, who says: "You don't have to serve foie gras to have a great restaurant; you don't have to make it complicated. Simple food tastes good. We have world-class rides and now we have world-class boardwalk food."

Ask for a table upstairs so you can overlook the amusement pier and the beach. If you're craving curly fries, you won't find them on the menu—but just ask your server and a batch will be delivered to your table, piping hot, from the Curley's Fries stand around the corner.

In February 2011, Jurusz competed in the tenth annual Men R' Cookin' event, benefitting the Boys and Girls Club of Atlantic City. He took home the award for best entrée in the professional division thanks to his Grilled Cape May Scallops with Cuban Spices and Chimichurri.

Golden Tilefish Sandwich

119

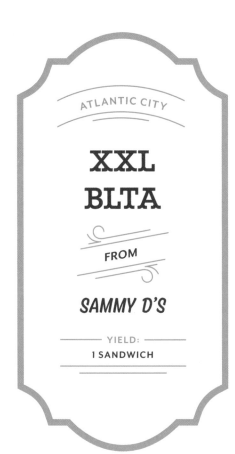

ATLANTIC CITY

XXL BLTA

FROM

SAMMY D'S

YIELD:
1 SANDWICH

The ideal time to make a BLT is in the summertime, when tomatoes are bursting with flavor. The folks at Sammy D's source theirs from Sunhaven Farms, updating the classic sandwich by adding freshly sliced avocados, lettuce varieties from Satur Farms, and a daub of chipotle mayonnaise.

½ cup mayonnaise

1 chipotle pepper in adobo sauce

1 teaspoon adobo sauce

Juice of ¼ lime

Salt, to taste

Freshly ground black pepper, to taste

2 ½-inch slices rustic country bread (sliced from the loaf lengthwise)

16 ⅛-inch slices bacon (such as Nueske's), cooked

2 cups seasonal mixed greens

2 Jersey tomatoes, sliced ¼ inch thick

1 avocado, sliced

2 sunny-side-up eggs (optional)

1. Make the chipotle mayonnaise: In a food processor, place mayonnaise, chipotle pepper, adobo sauce, and lime juice. Puree until smooth. Season to taste with salt and pepper.

2. Place bread on a baking sheet and toast under a broiler, turning once, for about 3 minutes.

3. Spread about 1 tablespoon of chipotle mayonnaise on one side of each bread slice. Layer bacon on one slice. On the other slice, layer greens and tomato; top with avocado and eggs (if using).

4. Season tomatoes and avocado with salt and pepper. Close sandwich, or serve it open-faced like they do at Sammy D's. Store leftover mayonnaise in an airtight container in the refrigerator.

CREDIT: Chef Sam DeMarco of Sammy D's

SAMMY D'S

This casual restaurant, bar, and lounge focusing on local ingredients and kicked-up classics is located in Harrah's Resort in Atlantic City. The restaurant's namesake, chef Samuel J. DeMarco (aka Sammy D), cut his teeth in the restaurant industry at the age of fifteen in New York City, where he worked with many prestigious chefs over the first decade of his impressive thirty-plus-year career. He opened his first restaurant, appropriately named First, in 1994 at the age of twenty-nine.

One of the most popular dishes at Sammy D's is the Lollipop Buffalo Wings, which were created at First back in the 1990s. The restaurant's over-the-top twists on simple foods quickly made Sammy D's a favorite Atlantic City destination. Speaking of over-the-top, if you're in the mood for something fun and attention grabbing, try the Sammy Splash, a fishbowl cocktail garnished with Swedish Fish, DeMarco's favorite candy.

DeMarco's career expanded onto the TV screen in 2014 when he debuted on the Travel Channel's *Chow Masters*. Along with his best friend, Frank Coraci (director of *The Wedding Singer*, *The Waterboy*, and *Blended*), DeMarco traveled the country, visiting off-the-map eateries serving unique twists on popular foods.

Born in Brooklyn, Sammy D moved to Las Vegas in 2008 with his family and opened the First Food and Bar at the Palazzo Hotel, where he oversaw all culinary operations. He now divides his time between Las Vegas and the East Coast.

121

THE
BLUEBERRY JACK BUBBA DOG

WITH

NEW JERSEY BLUEBERRY BBQ SAUCE

FROM

BUBBA DOGS

YIELD:
24 SERVINGS

What says New Jersey summer more than a hot dog or blueberries? Hot dogs with blueberry barbecue sauce! As Bubba Dogs owner Tim McNamara explains: "The sweet tang of the blueberries and barbecue sauce combined with the garlic saltiness of the hot dog could be the best thing you've never tasted." Try this dog with crumbled salt-and-vinegar potato chips. If you must scale down the recipe, still make a full batch of the sauce; it's ridiculously good on ribs, pork loin, and grilled chicken.

1 tablespoon butter

1 pint New Jersey blueberries, stems removed

2 tablespoons malt vinegar

1 tablespoon unsulfured molasses

1 16-ounce container your favorite barbecue sauce

24 hot dogs

24 hot dog buns

Monterey Jack cheese, to taste

1. In a medium saucepan over medium heat, melt butter and then add blueberries and stir for 2 minutes. Add vinegar and molasses, bring to a boil, and remove from heat.

2. Mash blueberries, being sure to leave some larger pieces. Add barbecue sauce and return saucepan to medium heat. Bring mixture to a boil, then reduce heat and simmer, stirring occasionally, for 5 minutes.

3. Cook hot dogs according to package directions. Place in buns and top with cheese. Top with barbecue sauce and serve. If you are making fewer than two dozen hot dogs, store leftover sauce in an airtight container in the refrigerator.

CREDIT: Bubba Dogs, 59th and the Beach, Sea Isle City, NJ

BUBBA DOGS

Since May 2002, Tim McNamara of Sea Isle City's Bubba Dogs has been repeating his mantra: "Toes in the sand with a Bubba Dog in hand."

If you hear the sound of a conch-shell horn blowing from the dunes, it's not an approaching pirate vessel—it's just Bubba Dogs announcing they're open for business. Act quickly to avoid the line. For a true Bubba Dog experience, try the "59th Street" (a hot dog topped with bacon, Cheez Whiz, barbecue sauce, and Herr's Potato Stix). And while you're there, be sure to grab a freshly squeezed lemonade, limeade, orangeade, or Arnold Palmer to quench your sun-induced thirst.

This little dog stand has won some big media awards and mentions from all over the region: *Philadelphia* magazine's Best of the Shore 2009, 2010, 2012, and 2014; *Coastal Living* magazine's "The Real Jersey Shore" 2011; *South Jersey Magazine*'s Best of the Shore 2010; Fox Philly's Best of the Shore 2008 and 2009; PHL 17 Hot List Best Hot Dog of South Jersey 2011; and *Suburban Family Magazine*'s Family Shore Guide 2011. Recently, *Philadelphia* magazine named Bubba Dogs one of the twelve "Must Eats" of the Jersey Shore.

Bubba Dogs is open Memorial Day through Labor Day. A second location operates in Glenside, Pennsylvania, under the name Jack Frost.

Owner Tim McNamara

123

BELMAR

LOBSTER ROLL

FROM

BRANDL

YIELD:
4 LOBSTER ROLLS

What's not to love about chunks of fresh lobster meat with the crispy crunch of celery on a buttery roll? Brandl has been serving this lobster roll for more than twenty-five years. Now you can have a bite of summer anytime, anywhere.

¾ cup mayonnaise

Squirt of freshly squeezed lemon juice

Freshly ground black pepper, to taste

Freshly ground sea salt, to taste

A couple pinches Old Bay seasoning

Dash Worcestershire sauce

Dash Tabasco sauce

¼ cup diced sweet onion

½ cup diced celery

1 pound shelled lobster meat in bite-size chunks

Softened butter

4 hot dog buns

1. In a medium bowl, combine mayonnaise, lemon juice, pepper, salt, Old Bay, Worcestershire sauce, and Tabasco. Taste and adjust seasoning as desired.

2. Stir in vegetables. Gently stir in lobster.

3. Butter both sides of hot dog buns. Toast them in a skillet or under the broiler. (This is easiest done on a griddle pan on the stovetop. Use a spatula to press the buns as the bottoms toast, then flip and toast the other sides.)

4. Fill toasted buns with lobster salad. Serve immediately.

CREDIT: Brandl

124

BELMAR

BRANDL

Belmar's Brandl has been a popular BYOB since 2002. Named after owner and executive chef Chris Brandl, this intimate fine dining establishment is known for its inventive menu and love of fresh seafood.

The most popular dish on Brandl's menu is the Lazy Lobster, which is poached in vanilla bean butter and served over asparagus risotto. Second in line are the crab cakes served over grilled corn remoulade. Or try oysters from 40 North Oyster Farm, clams from Virginia waters, or other locally sourced seafood. Check out Brandl's Facebook page on Fridays for the Fresh Catch Friday announcement. And be sure to order the dark chocolate soufflé in advance...trust me.

When Chef Brandl was twelve years old, his first job was as a dishwasher at the Farmingdale House, a beloved and highly rated restaurant in Monmouth County. He kept a close eye on well-known chef Toni Froio and dreamt of one day conjuring up his own kitchen magic. Brandl has been living his dream for the past fourteen years and shows no signs of slowing down. (From time to time, Brandl welcomes his old friend Toni Froio to act as visiting chef for special dinners, which usually sell out within a few hours.)

Voted Best Chef of Monmouth County by *Monmouth Health & Life*, Brandl is an active restaurateur. He is the founder of the Belmar Restaurant Tour and a participant in nearly every tasting event throughout Monmouth County, where you'll find him serving his famous crab balls. Brandl also regularly participates in Jersey Shore Restaurant Week.

125

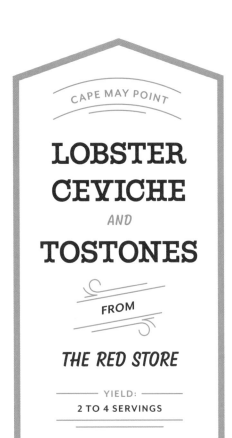

CAPE MAY POINT

LOBSTER CEVICHE
AND
TOSTONES

FROM

THE RED STORE

YIELD:
2 TO 4 SERVINGS

Ceviche is a popular Latin American appetizer in which pieces of fish are marinated in citrus juice. This version, which features fresh lobster, is served with fried plantain slices and plenty of fresh New Jersey produce. For an eye-catching presentation, arrange the lobster's head in the middle of the serving dish.

1 cup salt, plus more to taste

1 1½-pound live Maine lobster

3 jalapeños, seeded

1 bunch cilantro, chopped, divided

1 tablespoon honey

2 tablespoons lime juice

1 tablespoon lemon juice

2 tablespoons orange juice

1 garlic clove, peeled and sliced

1 shallot, peeled and sliced

½ cup extra-virgin olive oil

Ground black pepper, to taste

1 mango, peeled and diced

1 quart New Jersey strawberries, diced

1 red onion, diced

1 red bell pepper, diced

1 local cucumber, peeled and diced

1 chayote, grated

3 green plantains

1. Prepare lobster: Bring a large pot of water and salt to a boil over high heat. Add lobster, cover, and cook for 5 minutes. Use tongs to transfer to a bowl of ice water; let cool.

2. Separate the claws, head, and tail. Rinse the inside of the head under cold running water and set aside for presentation. Break claws with the back of a chef's knife and pull out all the meat. Repeat with knuckles. Cut tail in half lengthwise and pull out meat. Cut all lobster meat into bite-size pieces. Keep at room temperature if serving ceviche right away, or refrigerate until 5 minutes before serving and then bring to room temperature so the meat is not cold and tastes sweeter.

126

3. In a blender, combine jalapeños, half of the cilantro, honey, juices, garlic, shallots, and olive oil. Blend. Season with salt and pepper to taste.

4. Combine lobster, mangoes, strawberries, onions, bell peppers, the remaining cilantro, cucumbers, and chayote in a nonreactive stainless-steel bowl. Toss while drizzling in dressing. Let sit for 5 minutes before serving.

5. Make the tostones: Peel plantains and cut crosswise into 1-inch pieces. Bring a large pot of salted water to a boil. Add plantains and cook until fork-tender but not mushy. Drain. Crush plantains into patties using the inside of a plantain peel. Set aside.

6. Just before serving, brown plantain patties in a sauté pan with a little oil until both sides are crisp. Remove from heat and season with salt and pepper. Place ceviche in the middle of a serving plate and garnish with lobster head. Arrange tostones around ceviche. Serve and enjoy.

CREDIT: *Chef Lucas Manteca, Quahog's Seafood Shack, Stone Harbor, NJ, and The Red Store, Cape May Point, NJ*

THE RED STORE

The Red Store in Cape May Point is one part general store, one part casual coffee shop and café, and one part reservation-only restaurant helmed by James Beard nominee and chef Lucas Manteca and his wife, Deanna.

Born in Argentina, Manteca was a restaurateur by age twenty in Costa Rica. Today he draws upon South and Central American influences and his French Culinary Institute training to create some of the most inventive dishes on the Jersey Shore, using locally grown Jersey products.

Voted Top 10 in New Jersey by Zagat and one of the 25 Best Restaurants of 2014 by *New Jersey Monthly*, the Red Store offers breakfast, lunch, and dinner during peak season and an ongoing series of dinners for their "supper club" through fall, winter, and spring.

The Red Store breakfast menu is full of surprises, including Red Store Pancakes topped with crab, corn, and roasted poblano peppers. The dinner menu offers a daily empanada special and a list of seasonal produce sourced directly from Chef Lucas's personal farm. Speaking of farms, in 2015 the Mantecas became owners of Cape May Sea Salt Co., purveyors of high-quality, locally sourced and harvested salt for cooking and the table.

The Red Store is the latest of the Mantecas' restaurant ventures. They've also been the owners of Quahog's Seafood Shack in Stone Harbor, New Jersey, since 2008 (see page 91).

129

LOBSTER MAC AND CHEESE

FROM

LABRADOR LOUNGE

YIELD:
10 TO 15 SERVINGS

This comforting dish features pieces of rich lobster—tails and claws make for the best mac and cheese. Serve it as a side, family-style for a main course, or even in individual ramekins for a nice touch to any dinner party display.

1 pound macaroni, such as elbows, shells, or orecchiette (or lobster-shaped pasta if you can find it)

1 cup shredded cheddar cheese

1 cup shredded Monterey Jack cheese

1 cup cubed Swiss cheese

1 cup shredded Asiago cheese

3 cups heavy cream, divided

½ pound (1 cup) unsalted butter

¾ cup chopped fresh chives

½ cup sliced shallots

Sea salt, to taste

Freshly cracked black pepper, to taste

2 cups cooked and diced lobster meat

Grated Parmesan cheese, to taste

Bread crumbs, to taste

1. Cook pasta al dente according to package directions, transfer to a colander, and drain.

2. Bring a large pot of water to a boil over high heat. Fit a metal mixing bowl over it to create a double boiler. Add all cheeses (except Parmesan) and 1½ cups of the heavy cream.

3. Melt cheeses, stirring often to prevent burning. If mixture seems too stringy or clumpy, add some of the remaining cream. The texture should be velvety and a bit loose—the consistency of cheese soup.

4. Preheat oven to 350°F. In a sauté pan over medium heat, melt butter. Add chives, shallots, salt, and pepper. Cook, stirring, for 3 to 4 minutes, or until shallots are tender. Add lobster and cook, stirring, for 1 to 2 minutes.

5. In a large bowl, combine lobster mixture and pasta and stir. Slowly add as much cheese mixture as desired.

6. Transfer mixture to an oven-safe dish and top with Parmesan and bread crumbs. Bake for 12 minutes, or until browned on top and warm in the middle.

CREDIT: Marilyn Schlossbach, Labrador Lounge

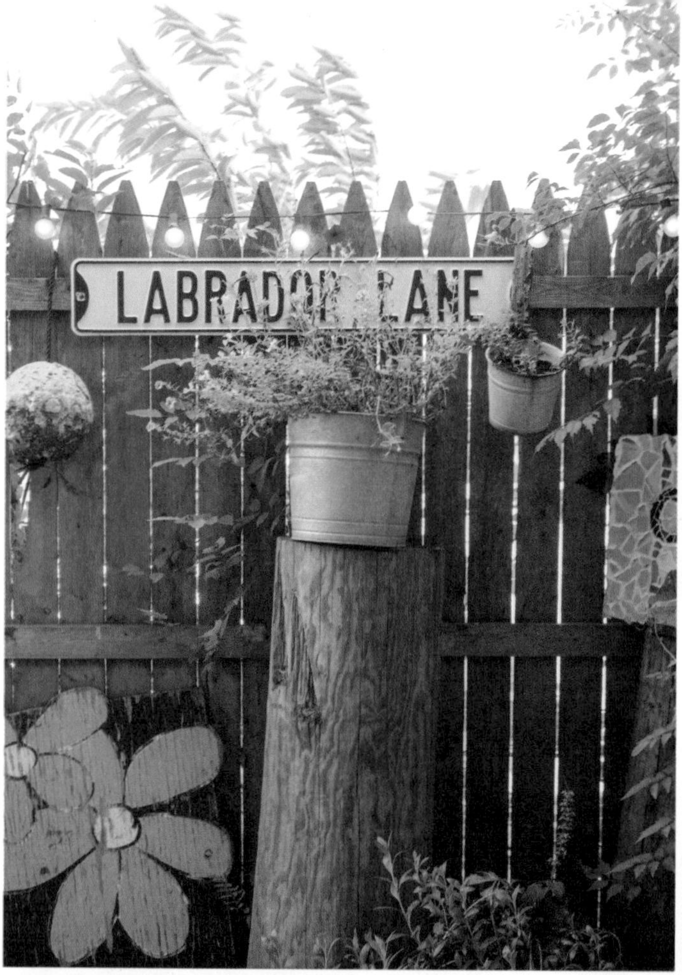
LABRADOR LANE

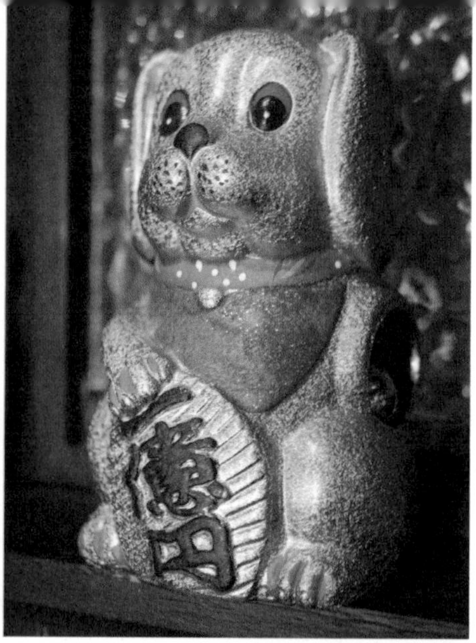

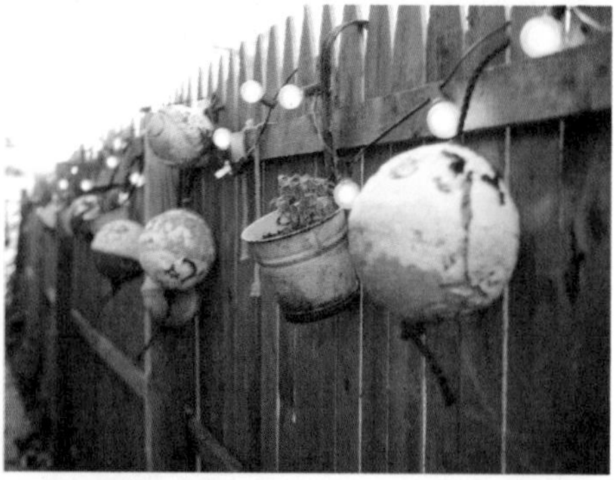

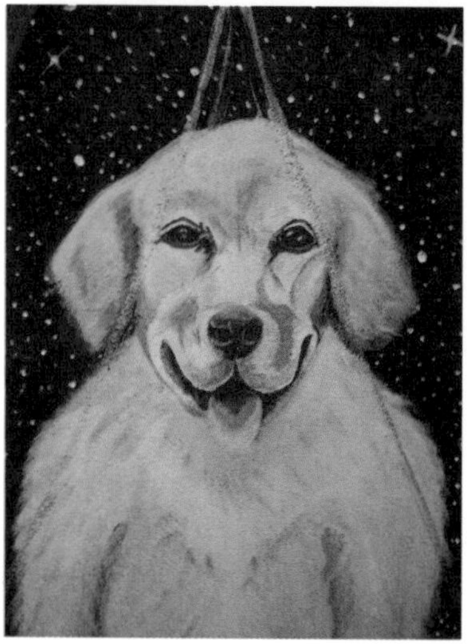

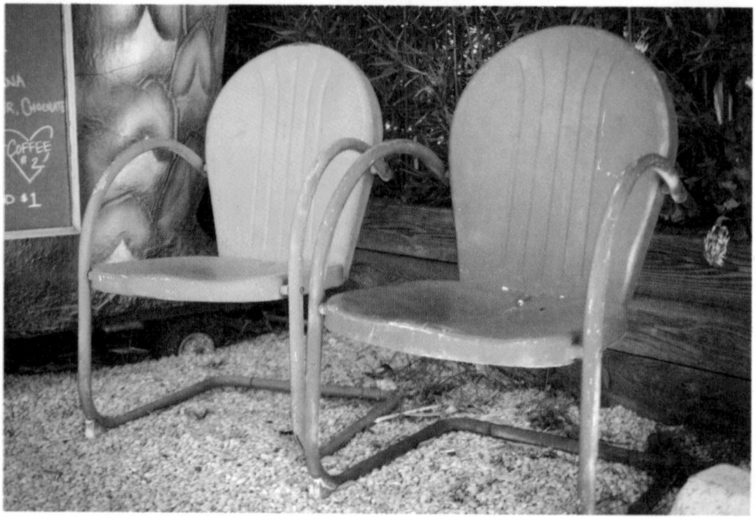

LABRADOR LOUNGE

The Labrador Lounge is restaurateur Marilyn Schlossbach's flagship restaurant in Normandy Beach. Established in 2003, it quickly became a local favorite and is well known throughout Ocean and Monmouth Counties for its fun, eclectic menu and incredibly fresh sushi.

The restaurant sources local ingredients based on seasonal availability. It also focuses on sourcing the freshest sustainable seafood. Labrador's lobster mac and cheese—a fan favorite since the beginning—is served with asparagus, cherry tomatoes, and scallions.

The indoor and outdoor seating areas are full of life, but the locals know to head to the sushi window on the side for a fun, private dining experience. Labrador also maintains standing summer reservations. One dedicated customer has had a reservation every Saturday night for years!

133

ATLANTIC CITY

LOBSTER THERMIDOR

FROM

KNIFE AND FORK INN

YIELD:
1 SERVING

This classic entree features chopped lobster tail meat, combined with sauce and other ingredients—here, a trio of flavorful mushrooms—that are traditionally spooned back into the empty lobster shell. It dates back fifty-plus years on the Knife and Fork Inn menu, where it remains because it represents an era and style that the restaurant holds dear.

1 2-pound freshly caught live lobster

1 ounce shallot, minced (about 2 small shallots)

1 ounce garlic, peeled and minced (about 6 garlic cloves)

¼ cup diced leeks (about ¼ large leek)

1 ounce cremini mushrooms, sliced (about ⅜ cup)

1 ounce shiitake mushrooms, sliced (about ⅜ cup)

1 ounce portobello mushrooms, sliced (about ⅜ cup)

2 tablespoons butter

2 fluid ounces sherry

1 tablespoon smooth Dijon mustard

1 tablespoon minced fresh tarragon

1¼ cups heavy cream

Salt, to taste

White pepper, to taste

4 tablespoons béarnaise sauce

1. Bring a large pot of water to a boil. Prepare a bowl of ice water; set aside. Add lobster to pot, cover, and cook for 2 minutes. (This will not fully cook the lobster, but it will allow you to remove the meat from the shell.) Immediately plunge lobster into ice water to stop cooking.

2. When lobster is cool, twist claw to remove from body. With the back of a chef's knife or meat tenderizer, split carapace along the top from head to tail. Be careful not to split the shell completely, because it will be the serving vessel.

3. Remove tail meat from shell and clean body shell as much as you want to. (Some people prefer to leave the roe and tomalley—the red eggs and soft green paste.) Carefully crack claws and knuckle and remove the meat. Cut meat into bite-size pieces and set aside.

4. In a large sauté pan over medium-high heat, sauté shallots, garlic, leeks, and mushrooms in butter until sauce has thickened slightly. Reduce heat to medium and simmer until vegetables have softened. Add sherry to deglaze pan, stirring to scrape bits from the bottom of the pan. Add mustard, tarragon, and cream. Season with salt and pepper to taste. Cook until sauce reduces and thickens slightly.

5. Add lobster meat to sauce and continue to simmer for 2 minutes.

6. Spread open lobster shell and place lobster mixture in cavity. Top with béarnaise sauce, and serve.

CREDIT: *Knife and Fork Inn*

KNIFE AND FORK INN

Knife and Fork Inn, located on the corner of Atlantic and Pacific Avenues in Atlantic City, is a landmark with a long and colorful past. When it was erected more than a century ago, it served as an exclusive men's drinking and dining club. The second floor was the Ladies Lounge (which it is still called today), where wives were required to wait while their husbands enjoyed the bar. Gambling (among "other things") took place on the third floor. During Prohibition, Knife and Fork was a well-known speakeasy; secret storage areas where the proprietors hid booze from the authorities still exist today. The restaurant has been featured in the HBO series *Boardwalk Empire* and on CNN's *Parts Unknown with Anthony Bourdain*.

Today, owner Frank Dougherty helms this historic restaurant, which he lovingly renovated in 2005 after purchasing it from longtime owner Mack Latz. The notorious third floor is now home to a glass-enclosed, temperature- and humidity-controlled wine "cellar," where the bottles of Knife and Fork's award-winning wine list are displayed. According to those in the know, the best seats in the house are in the Ladies Lounge, whose tables afford a beautiful ocean view.

Knife and Fork's menu spotlights an array of Jersey produce and seafood including local clams, Cape May oysters, day boat scallops, and local summer flounder. Executive chef James Huntzinger tells us that the lobster Thermidor is their best seller; locals will tell you to try the crabs (soft-shells throughout spring and summer, king crab in the fall). They have a direct relationship with the fishing vessel *Erla-N* in the Bering Sea, from which they source fresh Alaskan king crab.

137

"I can't let a summer go by without making some crab sauce—or gravy, depending on how you were raised to call it," says Joe Leone of Joe Leone's Italian Specialties. "This dish reminds me of being at my grandmother's house in Point Pleasant Beach. It's a nod to my nonna's famous crab sauce, and to my friend Nick Nicolosi's next-level version. My Aunt Grace makes the lobster sauce variation to this day."

POINT PLEASANT BEACH

SPAGHETTI AND CRABS

FROM

JOE LEONE'S ITALIAN SPECIALTIES

YIELD:
6 TO 8 SERVINGS

- 3 dozen 6- to 8-inch crabs, preferably Blue Points from the Jersey Bays, cleaned, divided
- 1 large onion, finely diced
- 6 carrots, small diced
- 1 tablespoon olive oil
- 1½ cups cooking sherry
- 6 cups homemade or your favorite store-bought tomato sauce
- 2 cups carrot juice
- 1 tablespoon granulated sugar
- ½ cup grated ricotta salata
- 1 teaspoon baking soda
- 1 bunch flat-leaf parsley, roughly chopped
- Seasonings such as garlic and/or oregano, to taste (optional)
- 2 pounds spaghetti
- 1 tablespoon extra-virgin olive oil
- Crushed red pepper flakes (optional)

1. Bring a large pot of water to a boil. Prepare a large bowl of ice water; set aside. Add 2 dozen crabs to pot, cover, and cook over medium heat for approximately 10 minutes, until red. Using tongs, transfer crabs to ice water to cool; reserve cooking water. Crack open shells and remove crabmeat. Set crabmeat aside in a bowl, discarding shells.

2. In a large pot, combine onions, carrots, and olive oil and cook over medium heat, uncovered, until carrots soften and onions are translucent. Add sherry. Cook for approximately

139

MAIN COURSES

2 minutes, until liquid has evaporated. Add the remaining 1 dozen crabs, tomato sauce, carrot juice, sugar, and ricotta salata. Gently simmer over low heat for 2 hours, stirring often.

3. Remove crabs from sauce and add baking soda (to remove the acid from the sauce). Continue to simmer for approximately 15 minutes, using a spoon to skim off foam from surface. Break the 1 dozen crabs into pieces. Add these (including their shells) and the reserved shelled crabmeat from step 1 to sauce. Stir and then add parsley. Season with garlic, oregano, or other seasonings to taste (if using).

4. Cover the opening of a large, empty pot with clean cheesecloth or a tea towel. Strain half of the reserved crab cooking water from step 1 into this pot. Remove cloth and fill the pot the rest of the way with fresh water, preferably bottled, and bring to a boil. Add spaghetti and cook al dente according to package instructions.

5. In a large bowl, mix spaghetti and sauce thoroughly. Drizzle with extra-virgin olive oil and red pepper flakes (if using). Serve and enjoy.

VARIATION: SPAGHETTI WITH LOBSTER SAUCE

Omit crabs. Add 1 pound live lobsters to the pot along with tomato sauce, carrot juice, sugar, and ricotta salata and cook for 7 to 8 minutes. Reduce heat to low and simmer sauce while preparing lobsters. Transfer lobsters to a cooling rack to cool slightly. Remove lobster meat from shells and set aside. Roughly chop lobster shells and add to sauce along with 2 boxes Pomi strained tomatoes. Simmer for 1 hour, stirring constantly. Add reserved lobster meat to sauce. Serve over al dente spaghetti.

CREDIT: *Chef-owner Joseph Leone Introna, Joe Leone's Italian Specialties*

JOE LEONE'S ITALIAN SPECIALTIES

Few Ocean County beachgoers pass by Joe Leone's Italian Specialties without stopping in for fresh mozzarella, house-made bread, and pasta sauce before they continue on to their seaside destinations.

Joe Leone's is the place to go for big party platters of chicken parmesan and penne with vodka sauce or mouthwatering Italian sandwiches on freshly baked bread. Prepared meals, which change daily, line the long glass-covered counter. Choices range from standards such as meatballs or sausage and peppers to specials like grilled pork chops di giambotta and quinoa with corn and basil. Overall, the business serves twenty-five to forty-five types of prepared dishes daily (depending on the time of year), including gluten-free options.

Open year-round, Joe Leone's practically shuts down Route 35 in Point Pleasant Beach during the holidays. Business on Christmas Eve is so busy that police are called in to help traffic keep moving. The line of patrons snakes out the door and down the street.

Joe Leone Introna himself is a local celebrity and a generous contributor to the community. Whether it's serving up spaghetti dinners at the local high school or helping an orphanage in Italy, Leone is ready to lend a hand—and some delicious food.

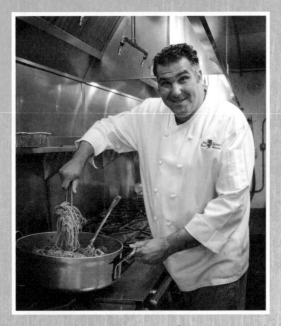

Owner Joe Leone Introna

141

Littleneck clams (also known as littlenecks) are hard-shelled clams with a diameter of less than two inches. They come about seven to ten to a pound. They're a New Jersey delicacy. If you can't find fresh herbs to pair with them, you may substitute dried herbs (about ¼ to ½ teaspoon of each).

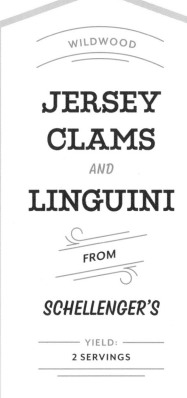

WILDWOOD

JERSEY CLAMS

AND

LINGUINI

FROM

SCHELLENGER'S

YIELD:
2 SERVINGS

8 to 12 ounces linguini

2 tablespoons olive oil, plus more for tossing

2 tablespoons butter

2 garlic cloves, chopped

Pinch crushed red pepper flakes

Salt, to taste

Ground black pepper, to taste

1 teaspoon fresh thyme leaves

1 teaspoon chopped fresh oregano

Splash white wine

½ cup clam juice or stock

About 24 Jersey littleneck clams (or more if they are small)

2 slices lemon

1 teaspoon chopped fresh parsley

1. Cook pasta three-quarters of the way, according to package directions. Rinse with cool water to stop cooking and toss with a little olive oil. Set aside. (The pasta will finish cooking in the sauce.)

2. In a large sauté pan over medium heat, heat 2 tablespoons oil and butter. Add garlic, red pepper flakes, salt, black pepper, thyme, and oregano and cook, stirring occasionally so the garlic doesn't burn, for 1 minute.

3. Add wine, stock, and clams and cook, covered, until clams open.

4. Add lemon slices and linguini and cook for about 2 minutes, tossing to mix. Top with parsley and serve.

CREDIT: Schellenger's Restaurant

143

SCHELLENGER'S

A trip to Wildwood isn't complete without a stop at Schellenger's Restaurant. Since 1979, Schellenger's has played a part in too many family vacations to count. Parents with cherished memories from their childhoods now make the pilgrimage with their own children, continuing the fun-filled tradition.

Chefs Glenn Dunleavy and Michael Salmon head up the kitchen. Dunleavy has been with the restaurant for more than two decades and revamps the menu each year. It's important to Schellenger's to keep things fresh while maintaining the nostalgia that people love.

Open May through September, the restaurant features a decor that is quintessential shore vacation: a wall-mounted marlin, hanging captain's wheels, and seagulls swinging overhead. Outside, boats, masts, buoys, flags, and even a giant lobster reside on their award-winning rooftop tableau. It's the first sign that you're about to have a really fun dining experience (not to mention the perfect spot for a selfie).

Since its opening, Schellenger's has been owned and operated by the Trivelis and Karros families, who purchased what was then a steakhouse and transformed it into the nautical destination it is today. The bar is known for its specialty cocktails, some of which come with a souvenir glass; standouts include the Captain's Specialty and the oyster shooter rimmed with Old Bay seasoning.

Menu favorites include the Fisherman's Feast, a whole lobster served with clams, mussels, shrimp, scallops, and fresh fish over linguini. Of course, you can't forget dessert, especially if the kids are along. Schellenger's selection of cakes, tiramisu, and pie du jour are fan favorites.

145

"At the Gables, we are lucky to have the Northeast's largest scallop-fishing fleet at the tip of our island," says owner Sondra Beninati. "We can buy large quantities of the best and freshest scallops directly from the dock at Viking Village. Scallops over risotto is a signature dish for us and our most popular entree." Here is a version for you to try at home.

SEARED

VIKING VILLAGE SCALLOPS

WITH

GRILLED CORN, ZUCCHINI, AND ROASTED TOMATOES

FROM

THE GABLES

— YIELD: —
4 TO 6 SERVINGS

3 ears fresh yellow corn, grilled

8 cups good chicken stock

3 tablespoons olive oil, divided

1 onion, diced

2 garlic cloves, minced

2 cups arborio rice

4 tablespoons butter, divided

½ cup dry white wine

12 to 16 jumbo scallops

Salt, to taste

Ground black pepper, to taste

1 large zucchini, diced

6 ripe plum tomatoes, halved, roasted at 300°F for 1 hour, and chopped

½ cup grated pecorino cheese

2 tablespoons fresh thyme

2 tablespoons chopped fresh Italian parsley

1 tablespoon gently chopped fresh basil

1. With a sharp knife, cut roasted corn kernels off cobs. In a large pot over medium-high heat, bring stock to a simmer and add corn cobs. Reduce heat to low to keep stock warm.

2. In a large skillet over medium heat, heat 1 tablespoon of the oil. Add onion and garlic and cook, stirring occasionally, for about 5 minutes, until translucent. Add rice and 2 tablespoons of the butter and sauté until rice begins to toast and stick a little to the pan. Add wine and cook, stirring, until wine is absorbed.

3. Add stock to rice, one ladleful at a time, until rice is just covered. Cook while stirring. When liquid is absorbed, add just enough stock to cover rice. Continue this process, stirring

after each addition of broth, until all liquid is absorbed, the consistency is thick, and the rice is al dente.

4. While rice is cooking, use a clean towel to pat scallops dry. Season with salt and pepper.

5. Preheat oven to 400°F. Heat a large ovenproof skillet over high heat until smoking hot and then add the remaining 2 tablespoons oil. Carefully add scallops one by one, searing each until golden brown on one side. When risotto is nearly finished, place skillet in oven to finish cooking scallops for about 5 minutes. (If they are small, you can skip this step. They will cook in the pan completely.)

6. After about 15 to 20 minutes, the risotto should be slightly firm and creamy. Add corn kernels, zucchini, and roasted tomatoes. Season to taste with salt and pepper. Cook briefly, stirring occasionally, until zucchini is just tender.

7. Stir in pecorino, the remaining 2 tablespoons butter, and herbs. Arrange scallops on risotto and serve.

CREDIT: *The Gables Historic Inn*

THE GABLES

You'll know you're in for a special evening before even setting foot inside the Gables when you're greeted by the cheerful garden of pink petunias and yellow daisies, porch-hanging geraniums, and purple irises lining the winding path to the front door.

Behind that door is a 1932 Steinway Model M baby grand piano, at which local pianist Steve Kramer performs beautiful dinner music most Saturday nights. The lovingly restored 1892 Victorian home was purchased in 2005 by Sondra and Steve Beninati—"to save it from a wrecking ball," the owners confessed. At the time, it was known as the Green Gables. The new owners "banished the green paint, slapped on a coat of sunny yellow, and reincarnated it as the Gables."

Chef Richard Diemer puts out inspired dishes spotlighting Jersey produce, local fish, and seafood from Viking Village in Barnegat. The Gables menu is not your standard Shore fare. The scallops recipe they generously contributed here is their most popular dish. Insiders will tell you to order the S'mores Tartlette for dessert.

Deciding on where to sit could present a dilemma. You'll have to choose among the inviting front porch overlooking the bustling beach traffic, the beautifully appointed interior dining rooms with their candlelit tables, or the backyard garden patio with sparkling fountain and copious flowers. Whichever you choose, you're in for a memorable meal.

Over the years, the restaurant and inn have racked up many awards, including an excellent rating from TripAdvisor and a nod as one of Zagat's Top Places to Stay in the US. It was also named Most Romantic Restaurant in Southern New Jersey by *New Jersey Monthly*.

PANKO-PARMESAN-CRUSTED NEW JERSEY SCALLOPS

OVER

ARUGULA PESTO

FROM

THE CRAB'S CLAW INN

YIELD:
2 SERVINGS

Many different types of fish, including halibut, snapper, and flounder, are delicious in this recipe (shown opposite). You can make the pesto in advance. For an impressive presentation, garnish with grilled prosciutto-wrapped asparagus: Wrap 6 lightly blanched asparagus spears in prosciutto, drizzle lightly with olive oil, and grill just until soft.

2 large handfuls arugula

1 ounce garlic (about 5 medium-sized cloves)

½ cup almonds or walnuts, toasted

½ cup olive oil

2 ounces grated Parmesan cheese (about ½ cup), divided

1 cup panko bread crumbs

Salt, to taste

Ground black pepper, to taste

16 ounces scallops, muscle removed

½ cup butter, melted

1. Make the pesto: In a food processor or blender combine arugula, garlic, nuts, and oil and process until consistency is a smooth paste. Transfer to a small bowl and stir in about two-thirds of the Parmesan.

2. Preheat oven to 450°F. Combine panko, the remaining Parmesan, salt, and pepper. Place scallops in a small baking dish. Press panko mixture onto scallops and drizzle with melted butter.

3. Bake for about 25 minutes, depending on size of scallops. They should be firm to the touch when cooked.

4. To serve, spread a small amount of pesto on each of two plates. Arrange scallops on top of pesto.

CREDIT: The Crab's Claw Inn

THE CRAB'S CLAW INN

Since 1979, Louise Hammer and her husband, Sam, have been serving hungry locals and seasonal guests at their Lavallette restaurant, the Crab's Claw Inn. Today it's a real family affair, with daughter Shannon, a teacher, working in the dining room during summers; son Sam, a professional surfer, handling the craft beer menu; and son-in-law Craig Korb heading up the kitchen.

The restaurant was nominated for a Taste award in 2015 for outstanding restaurant in the Bar/Pub category. It offers an impressive selection of bottled imported beers in addition to local craft brews on tap. The well-worn bar seats approximately thirty-five people, and you'll find a second bar upstairs.

Living up to its name, the Crab's Claw Inn serves up an array of crab-focused dishes and fish delicacies. Sam Senior personally cleans and prepares almost all the fresh fish that comes through the door. The Hammers are passionate about sourcing local produce and foods. Every October they host a Jersey Fresh Wine dinner, for which the folks from the New Jersey Department of Agriculture come bearing all kinds of goodies to share with guests.

Panko-Parmesan-Crusted New Jersey Scallops over Arugula Pesto

151

GRILLED JERSEY TOMATOES

WITH

DAY BOAT SCALLOPS, ASPARAGUS, CORN, AND GORGONZOLA

FROM

OYSTER CREEK INN

YIELD:
4 SERVINGS

"I like running this dish [shown opposite] as a special in the summer when Jersey vegetables—in this case asparagus, corn, and tomatoes—are at their best," says Oyster Creek Inn chef Scott Kuppel. "It features all things Garden State, from the scallops to the produce."

1 bunch medium-size Jersey summer asparagus, ends trimmed

3 ears Jersey Silver Queen corn, husked

1 pound New Jersey day boat scallops (10 to 20 scallops)

2 large beefsteak tomatoes, sliced in quarters

½ cup olive oil

Salt, to taste

Ground black pepper, to taste

4 ounces crumbled Gorgonzola or blue cheese

½ cup balsamic vinegar (optional)

1. In a medium pot over high heat, bring 1 quart water to a boil. Add asparagus and blanch for 2 minutes. Remove with tongs and run under cold water to halt cooking. Place on a towel.

2. Heat grill to 425°F. Place corn on grill and char on all sides. Remove and let cool slightly; keep grill turned on. With a sharp knife, cut kernels from cob. Set kernels aside.

3. Brush scallops, tomatoes, and asparagus with olive oil and season with salt and pepper. Place scallops on grill for 2 minutes. Flip scallops and add tomato slices. Grill for 2 minutes and flip tomato slices. Move scallops to low heat. Place asparagus on grill. Top tomato slices with Gorgonzola and let it melt. Continue to cook asparagus until nicely charred.

4. To serve: Place 2 tomato slices on each plate. Place 2 scallops on each tomato slice. Lay asparagus between tomatoes. Garnish with corn kernels. Splash with balsamic vinegar, if desired, and serve.

CREDIT: Executive chef Scott Kuppel

OYSTER CREEK INN

Established in 1938 as a place for local fishermen to eat and sleep, the Oyster Creek Inn originally stood across the street from its current location. It was moved in the 1960s, after a bad storm wiped it out, to where it sits today, thirteen feet above Oyster Creek. It offers panoramic views of the Edwin B. Forsythe National Wildlife Refuge and Great Bay.

The Kuppel family purchased the restaurant in 1946, and it has been in the family ever since. Father William Kuppel is the owner. Chef Scott Kuppel runs the kitchen, and you can find his brother John tending at the legendary boat bar.

The restaurant has a dock that can accommodate boats up to sixty feet long, although they have to think about the tides. The average boat need not worry. Come by boat or by car, but get there before 5 p.m. on weekends. It's open year-round, but hours vary by season.

The restaurant has garnered its share of awards, including numerous Best of the Press honors from the *Press of Atlantic City*. It was featured in an episode of *Diners, Drive-ins & Dives*, in which Guy Fieri fell in love with the Clams Mexicali.

Grilled Jersey Tomatoes

153

SEARED SCALLOPS

WITH

RED PEPPER COULIS

FROM

THE LOBSTER HOUSE

YIELD:
4 SERVINGS

Some of the many scallops caught off the coast of Cape May are unloaded at the Lobster House. Get scallops as fresh as you can for this recipe, and serve it with garlic mashed potatoes.

4 red bell peppers, halved and seeded

Olive or canola oil, for roasting

Salt, to taste

Ground black pepper, to taste

1 red onion, peeled and sliced

1 leek

1 10.5-ounce can low-sodium chicken broth

6 slices uncooked bacon, diced

12 button mushrooms, sliced

2 pounds scallops (20 to 40 scallops, depending on size)

1. Preheat oven to 400°F. Rub peppers with oil, salt, and pepper and arrange them and onions on a baking tray. Roast for 15 minutes, until peppers are slightly charred. Meanwhile, slice leeks (white parts only) and rinse in a bowl of water.

2. Remove tray from oven (leave oven on). Put peppers in a plastic bag and tie it closed. Let cool. Remove charred skin; it should come off easily. Transfer peppers and onions to a blender and puree on high speed. While blending, add chicken broth—a little at a time—as needed to make the puree smooth.

3. Heat a large sauté pan over medium-high heat and cook bacon until crisp. Add leeks and mushrooms and cook for about 5 minutes, until soft. Add pepper puree and toss with leek mixture until hot.

4. Place a 10-inch sauté pan over medium high heat and add 2 tablespoons oil. When pan is hot, add half the scallops and sauté for about 3 minutes, until browned. Turn scallops over with a spatula and brown the other side for another 3 minutes. Transfer to a baking sheet and repeat with remaining scallops. Transfer to oven and bake for 8 minutes.

5. Spoon warm coulis onto plates, top with scallops, and serve.

CREDIT: The Lobster House

THE LOBSTER HOUSE

Open seven days a week year-round, the Lobster House on Fisherman's Wharf in Cape May Harbor is probably one of the most well-known and beloved restaurants in the Garden State. Established in 1954, the restaurant has served generations of vacationers to the historic Shore destination.

Commercial fisherman Wally and wife Marijane Laudeman founded the institution. It was home to their children Keith and Donna, who grew up playing and fishing off of their father's dock. Great-grandfather Cap Johnson owned party fishing boats back in the 1920s and '30s. Today Keith, in addition to running the restaurant, is president of the Cold Spring Fish and Supply Company, which ships fresh-caught seafood all over the world.

For a memorable dining experience, board the 130-foot-long authentic Grand Banks sailing vessel the *Schooner American*, which is moored dockside. It serves as an outdoor cocktail lounge with a full bar, lunch menu, and Lobster House specialty appetizers during the evening. Sip the signature Orange Crush cocktail for that summer-in-a-glass experience.

The take-out shop offers a more casual dining setting, plus the option to take home the catch of the day and grill it yourself. They also offer ready-made soups. The Raw Bar evokes an old waterfront boathouse and is filled with historic Cape May fishing memorabilia. And finally there is the main dining room, with knotty pine paneling, tablecloths, and the occasional mermaid and duck decoys to round out your seashore experience.

155

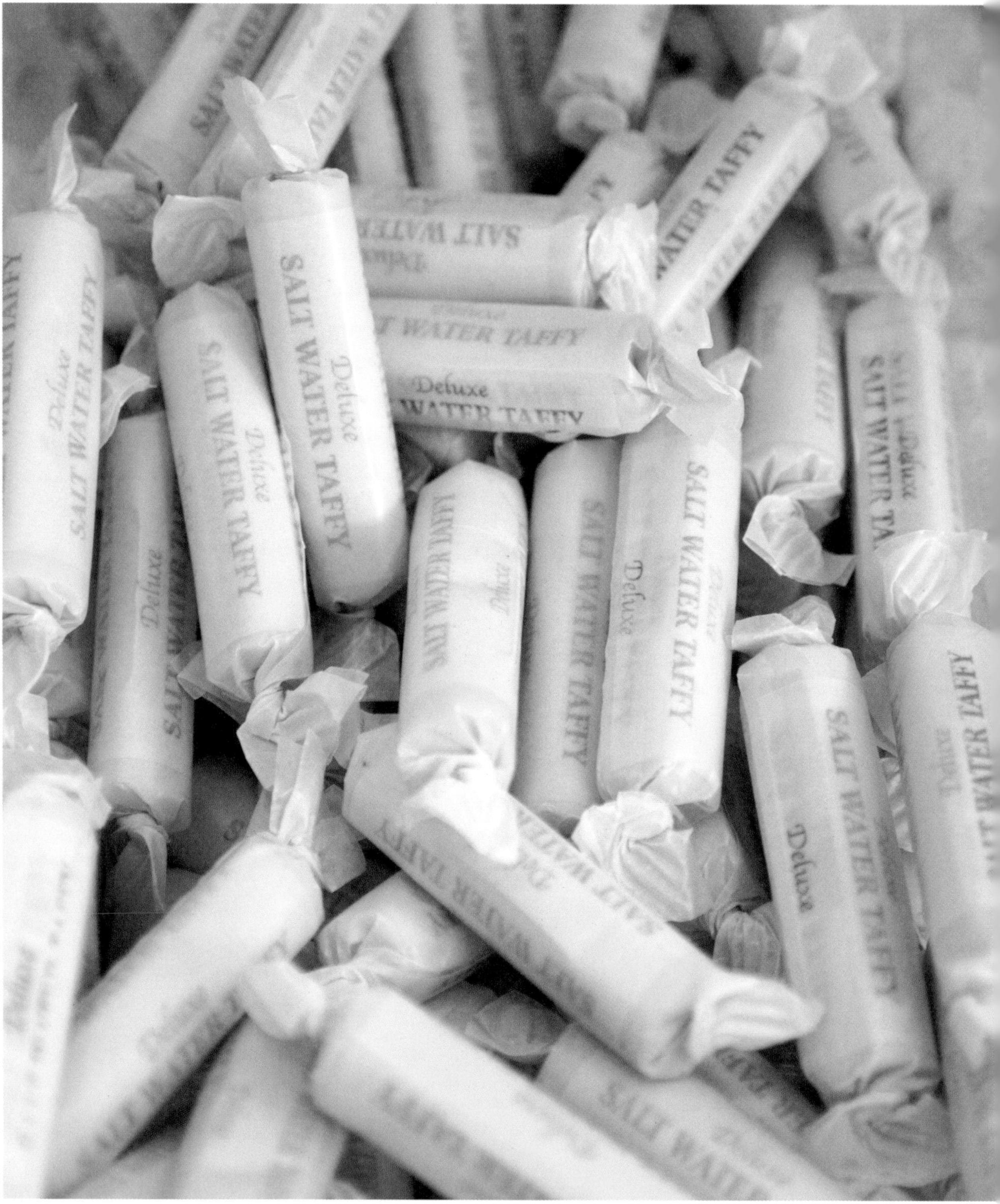
Deluxe
SALT WATER TAFFY

DESSERTS

ASBURY PARK

BLUEBERRY COBBLER

FROM

TALULA'S

YIELD:
1 9-BY-13-INCH COBBLER,
ABOUT 10 TO 12 SERVINGS

The last thing you want to do in the summer is cook over a hot stove making overly fussy desserts. Fortunately, this cobbler (shown opposite) is as easy as making a quick butter cake batter and scattering fresh blueberries over top. All the magic happens in the oven.

3 cups organic all-purpose flour

3 tablespoons baking powder

1½ teaspoons kosher salt

1½ cups unsalted butter, softened, plus more for greasing pan

2¼ cups organic cane sugar

3 teaspoons vanilla extract

6 large eggs

4 pints organic Jersey blueberries

4 tablespoons turbinado sugar

1. Preheat oven to 350°F. Butter a 9-by-13-inch cake pan or half hotel pan. Whisk together flour, baking powder, and salt and set aside.

2. With an electric hand mixer or a stand mixer fitted with a paddle attachment, cream butter and cane sugar on medium-high speed until light and fluffy. Turn mixer to low speed and add vanilla and then eggs, one at a time. Turn off mixer and use a rubber spatula to scrape down the sides of the bowl. Turn mixer to medium-high speed and beat mixture until eggs are fully incorporated and fluffy.

3. Turn mixer to low speed and gently stir in dry ingredients until just combined. Pour batter into prepared pan and smooth the top with a spatula. Scatter blueberries on top and sprinkle with turbinado sugar.

4. Bake for about 35 to 40 minutes, or until a cake tester, toothpick, or butter knife inserted into the center comes out clean. Serve and enjoy with a scoop of your favorite ice cream.

CREDIT: Talula's, Asbury Park

TALULA'S

Talula's burst onto the Asbury Park food scene in late 2014. Husband-and-wife team Shanti and Steve Mignogna, owners and chefs, quickly became a welcome addition to the downtown community.

Talula's is known for its small but exciting menu that follows the seasons. The cobbler you see here is served from early summer until the end of the Jersey blueberry season. Talula's most popular dish is the Beekeeper's Lament Pizza. Made with sourdough, all-organic flour from Central Milling and Farmer Ground in Trumansburg, New York, it is topped with San Marzano tomato sauce, house-made mozzarella, hot sopressata, Calabrian chili oil, and a drizzle of local honey after it comes out of the oven.

Regulars will tell you that the doughnuts offered at weekend brunch are not to be missed. Served between 10:30 a.m. and 4 p.m. (or until they run out), they are always fried to order.

The best seat in the house is found at the round table by the window; it was made by Steve's brother Paul Mignogna, a Brooklyn-based furnituremaker. According to Shanti, "It always gets the perfect light. People always seem to stay a little while longer when they're gathered around it."

Talula's wasted no time scooping up accolades. In 2015, it was named New and Notable by *New Jersey Monthly* magazine, Top 25 Pizzas by NJ.com, and Reader's Choice Best Pizza and Best New Restaurant by Monmouth Health and Life.

Left: Blueberry cobbler; right: owners and chefs Shanti and Steve Mignogna

KEY LIME PIE

FROM

INLET CAFÉ

YIELD:
1 9-INCH PIE

This summer classic is inspired by the Lentz family's travels throughout South Florida and the Keys. It's delicious and simple—you can even use a store-bought graham cracker crust instead of making your own.

CRUST

1½ cups graham cracker crumbs

⅓ cup granulated sugar

6 tablespoons salted butter or margarine, melted

Pinch ground cinnamon

FILLING

1 14-ounce can sweetened condensed milk

3 egg yolks

½ cup Nellie & Joe's Key West Lime Juice (available in most supermarkets)

1 teaspoon grated lime zest

TO SERVE

Whipped cream

Fresh lime slice

1. Preheat oven to 350°F. In a mixing bowl, mix graham cracker crumbs, sugar, butter, and cinnamon until well combined. Press mixture into an 8- or 9-inch pie plate. Set aside.

2. In another bowl, combine condensed milk, egg yolks, key lime juice, and lime zest. Blend with a whisk until smooth. Pour filling into pie shell and bake for 15 minutes. Refrigerate well before serving, at least 3 hours. Garnish with fresh whipped cream and a fresh lime slice.

CREDIT: Inlet Café

INLET CAFÉ

The Inlet Café, run by the second generation of the Lentz family, celebrated its fiftieth year in 2015. Leslie and Mildred Lentz established this riverside restaurant in 1966, choosing the name because of rumors that an inlet through to Sandy Hook was coming. Although the rumors never became fact, patrons can enjoy a stunning view of the Shrewsbury River and Sandy Hook from the spacious deck. It's the perfect spot to take in a sunset.

For many years, the Inlet Café was famous for their "all-you-can-eat steamers." Unfortunately, those days are gone, but they still serve steamers, along with the very popular Baja fish tacos and crab-encrusted grouper. Inlet's lobster bisque won Best Lobster Bisque in the Shore Chef Cookoff sponsored by the *Star-Ledger*.

Here's a secret only locals know: if you catch a fish, bring it to the restaurant and chef David Buzzelli will prepare it for you. While you're waiting, enjoy the house-made sangria, which comes frozen or on the rocks. The Inlet is also known for its infamous happy hour. The restaurant closes each year in December and reopens on St. Patrick's Day.

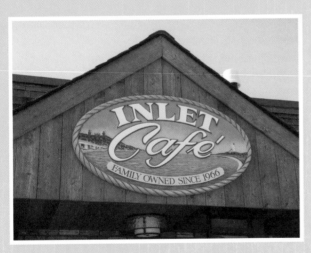

161

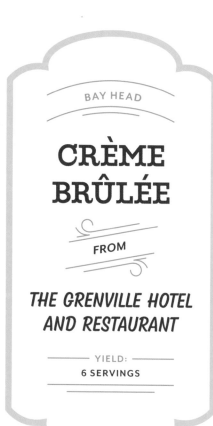

CRÈME BRÛLÉE

FROM

THE GRENVILLE HOTEL AND RESTAURANT

YIELD:
6 SERVINGS

This thick, custardy crème brûlée (shown opposite) is the Grenville Hotel and Restaurant's number one dessert throughout the year. It can be served cold or warm—just microwave it for 30 to 45 seconds before torching the sugar. The liqueur adds an extra layer of flavor.

1 egg plus 4 egg yolks

½ cup granulated sugar

3 cups heavy cream

1 teaspoon pure vanilla extract

1 tablespoon liqueur such as Grand Marnier or Baileys Irish cream, optional

About 1½ teaspoons brown sugar, for topping

1. Preheat oven to 350°F. With an electric mixer on low speed (or using a whisk), mix egg, egg yolks, and granulated sugar until combined.

2. In a medium saucepan over medium-high heat, warm cream almost to a boil. Slowly add to egg mixture while continuing to mix or whisk. Add vanilla and liqueur (if using).

3. Pour into six 8-ounce ramekins or a shallow ovenproof bowl. Place ramekins in a baking pan and pour warm water to nearly the top of the ramekins. Cover pan with foil and bake for 30 to 45 minutes. To check for doneness, gently shake a ramekin to ensure custard has set (is not watery).

4. Remove ramekins from baking pan, let cool to room temperature, and refrigerate to chill completely, about 2 hours.

5. Remove ramekins from refrigerator and let sit at room temperature for about an hour. Sprinkle brown sugar evenly onto custard, crushing chunks with your fingertips. Use a kitchen torch to caramelize the sugar. Serve right away.

CREDIT: Grenville

THE GRENVILLE HOTEL AND RESTAURANT

Founded in 1890, the Grenville Hotel has lived through many storms and changes throughout more than a century on the Jersey Shore. One of the true grandes dames of the Victorian era, the hotel was constructed by Wycoff Applegate, builder of the Bay Head Yacht Club. The restaurant was established in 1987.

Chef Harry Typaldos now leads the line at the Grenville. The daily fresh fish special is always in high demand, and the most popular dish is a tie between the blackened ribeye and the artichoke-encrusted sea bass.

The Grenville is open year-round, so you can enjoy al fresco dining on the veranda in summer or a warm cozy spot in front of the fireplace in winter. The hotel is within walking distance of all the great shopping and beaches in Bay Head. This small, quaint community offers plenty to do, but for attractions such as roller coasters and tiki bars, head to the next town over, Point Pleasant Beach.

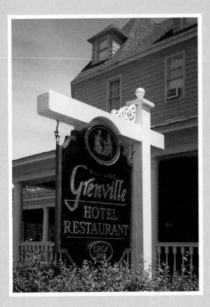

Crème brûlée

163

Panna cotta (Italian for "cooked cream") is one of those desserts that's difficult to resist during the long days of summer. It's also simple to make, beautiful to look at (especially garnished), and amazing to eat.

ASBURY PARK

PEACH PANNA COTTA

FROM

PORTA

YIELD:
APPROXIMATELY 9
8-OUNCE SERVINGS

PANNA COTTA

7 sheets silver-grade gelatin (look for it at gourmet food stores or online)

6 ½ cups heavy cream

1¼ cups granulated sugar

½ cup Greek yogurt

1 vanilla bean, split lengthwise, seeds scraped out

2 cups goat's milk

⅓ teaspoon kosher salt

PEACHES

6 ripe peaches, peeled and finely diced

6 large basil leaves, cut into a chiffonade

½ cup granulated sugar

1 teaspoon kosher salt

1 tablespoon freshly squeezed lemon juice

1. In a large bowl filled with 7 cups water, soak gelatin for about 5 to 10 minutes, until soft. Meanwhile, in a heavy-bottomed pot over medium heat, warm heavy cream, sugar, yogurt, and vanilla bean pod and seeds until solids have dissolved and mixture is hot but not boiling.

2. Reduce heat to low and add gelatin to pot. Stir constantly until gelatin is dissolved. Add goat's milk and salt. Stir.

3. Pour mixture through a fine-mesh strainer to separate lumps. Pour into molds, small bowls, or mason jars and refrigerate until set, about 1 to 2 hours (up to 4 hours or preferably overnight if you want to remove panna cotta from molds). Panna cotta should be firm but not creamy.

4. In a bowl, mix together peaches, basil, sugar, salt, and lemon juice. Serve over panna cotta.

CREDIT: Porta

165

PORTA

Founded in 2011, Porta was the brainchild of Meg Brunette, one of the four partners in Smith. The name of this authentic Neapolitan pizzeria in Asbury Park comes from an Italian proverb about a would-be monk named Martin, who had to transcribe the sentences *"Porta patens esto. Nulli claudatur honesto"* (rough translation: "May the door always be open. May it never be closed to honest people"). Problem is, Martin put the period in the wrong place, changing the meaning to "May the door never be open. May it be closed to honest people." The story emphasizes the need for attention to detail, which clearly the team at Porta have taken to heart. And it's paid off: The *New York Times* rated Porta "excellent."

Chef Rob Santello incorporates Jersey fresh ingredients throughout the year. Porta's seasonal menus are founded on a strong tie to local farms and showcase this bounty in everything from pizza toppings and salads to desserts.

Porta is housed in a building originally called the Student Prince; according to legend, it's where Bruce Springsteen first met Clarence Clemons. The restaurant's atmosphere is whimsical, with an array of doors, all different sizes and colors, adorning the walls. Outside in "Porta Park," you can hang out at picnic tables, listen to live bands, and play bocce.

CONTRIBUTOR DIRECTORY

AMA RISTORANTE AT DRIFTWOOD (page 80)
1485 Ocean Avenue
Sea Bright, NJ 07760
www.amaristorante.com

THE ARLINGTON (page 95)
1302 Long Beach Boulevard
Ship Bottom, NJ 08008
www.arlingtonlbi.com

AVENUE (page 72)
23 Ocean Avenue
Long Branch, NJ 07740
www.leclubavenue.com

BAHRS LANDING (page 86)
2 Bay Avenue
Highlands, NJ 07732
www.bahrslanding.com

BEACH TAVERN (page 115)
33 West Street
Monmouth Beach, NJ 07750
www.beachtavern.net

BLACK-EYED SUSANS (page 77)
7801 Long Beach Boulevard
Harvey Cedars, NJ 08008
www.blackeyedsusanslbi.com

THE BLUE PIG TAVERN (page 111)
200 Congress Place
Cape May, NJ 08204
www.caperesorts.com

BRANDL (page 124)
703 Belmar Plaza
Belmar, NJ 07719
www.brandlrestaurant.com

BRICKWALL TAVERN AND DINING ROOM (page 38)
522 Cookman Avenue
Asbury Park, NJ 07712
www.brickwalltavern.com

BROAD STREET DINER (page 16)
83 Broad Street
Keyport, NJ 07735
www.83broadstreetdiner.com

BUBBA DOGS (page 122)
59th Street and the Beach
Sea Isle City, NJ 08243

THE BUTTERED BISCUIT (page 14)
700 Main Street
Bradley Beach, NJ 07720
www.thebutteredbiscuitcafe.com

CHEF MIKE'S ABG (page 34)
10 Central Avenue
South Seaside Park, NJ 08752
www.chefmikesabg.com

THE CHICKEN OR THE EGG (page 26)
207 North Bay Avenue
Beach Haven, NJ 08008
www.492fowl.com

THE COMMITTED PIG (page 18)
168 Main Street
Manasquan, NJ 08736
www.thecommittedpig.com

THE CRAB'S CLAW INN (page 150)
601 Grand Central Avenue
Lavallette, NJ 08735
www.thecrabsclaw.com

THE DIVING HORSE (page 68)
2109 Dune Drive
Avalon, NJ 08202
www.thedivinghorseavalon.com

DOCK'S OYSTER HOUSE (page 106)
2405 Atlantic Avenue
Atlantic City, NJ 08401
www.docksoysterhouse.com

THE EBBITT ROOM (page 66)
Virginia Hotel and Cottages
25 Jackson Street
Cape May, NJ 08204
www.caperesorts.com

FRATELLO'S RESTAURANT (page 43)
810 The Plaza
Sea Girt, NJ 08750
www.fratellosrestaurant.com

THE GABLES (page 147)
212 Centre Street
Beach Haven, NJ 08008
www.gableslbi.com

THE GRENVILLE HOTEL & RESTAURANT (page 162)
345 Main Avenue
Bay Head, NJ 08742
www.thegrenville.com

INLET CAFÉ (page 160)
3 Cornwall Street
Highlands, NJ 07732
www.inletcafe.com

IRON ROOM RESTAURANT (page 70)
648 North Albany Avenue
Atlantic City, NJ 08401
www.acbottlecompany.com/food

JOE LEONE'S ITALIAN SPECIALTIES (page 139)
510 Route 35 South
Point Pleasant Beach, NJ 08742
www.joeleones.com

ABOUT THE AUTHOR

A born and bred Jersey Shore native, Deborah Smith is the founder of JerseyBites.com, a food blog launched in 2007 that reports on food news and restaurant reviews in the Garden State. The site is now home to more than thirty food writers (known as the Biters) and engages with over 30,000 fans daily on all the major social media channels.

In her role as executive editor of *Jersey Bites*, Deborah served as a founding member of Jersey Shore Restaurant Week and, most recently, as a judge for Jersey Shore Restaurant Week's Taste Awards. Over the years, she has served as a judge for numerous food competitions and been invited to speak about food in New Jersey both live and on the air. She is a proud mom to two amazing teenage boys and resides in Point Pleasant Beach with her "better half" Peter and their two dogs.

ABOUT THE PHOTOGRAPHER

Tom Clarke is an editorial and commercial photographer best known for location portraiture, architecture, and food photography. He is a contributor to such publications as *Self Magazine*, *Fitness Magazine*, *Edible Jersey*, PA and NJ *Meetings+Events* magazines, *Bucks Life*, *Mainline Magazine*, and more, and his product photography can be seen on packaging in stores around the world. Tom and his wife, Heather, live just outside Princeton, New Jersey, where they hike, cook, binge-watch TV, travel, and volunteer at their local food bank. For more, visit thomasrobertclarke.com.

ACKNOWLEDGMENTS

Thank you to all of my wonderful friends and family (too many to mention here) who have supported me throughout my food writing journey. I've heard and continue to hear a lot of "I'm so proud of you," which means the world to me, even at my age.

I'd like to thank my good friend Jim Flynn, president of Jersey Shore Restaurant Week, for helping me corral so many of the restaurants in this book. I would also like to thank my business partner and friend, Mike Ciavolino, for his help in lining up local restaurants in his community.

Thank you to Rachel Bozek, *Jersey Bites* editor, for keeping that ship sailing along smoothly while I dove into this project, and thank you to all of our *Jersey Bites* contributors, without whom the blog would not exist. And thank you to Tiffany Hill, cookbook editor extraordinaire, for the fantastic guidance, encouragement, and way more assistance than I ever expected. There would not be a *Jersey Shore Cookbook* without her.

To my two gorgeous teenaged boys, Tanner and Connor, I want to thank you for eating a little too much takeout as Mom worked on this book and for one day being super proud of your mom, the author. I realize that's asking a bit too much right now. And, to my bestie, Jill Van Schoick, thank you for getting even more excited than I do over my food adventures. I bet you're excited to see your name here, aren't you?

And, last but not least, thank you to my better half, Peter Culos, who has been and continues to be the biggest cheerleader and fan of my life since high school. He's my partner in crime and a fantastic writer. Your encouragement and words of advice mean the world to me.

METRIC CONVERSIONS

Use these rounded equivalents to convert between the traditional American systems used to measure volume and weight and the metric system.

VOLUME

AMERICAN	IMPERIAL	METRIC
¼ tsp		1.25 ml
½ tsp		2.5 ml
½ tbsp (1½ tsp)		7.5 ml
1 tbsp (3 tsp)		15 ml
¼ cup (4 tbsp)	2 fl oz	60 ml
⅓ cup (5 tbsp)	2½ fl oz	75 ml
½ cup (8 tbsp)	4 fl oz	125 ml
⅔ cup (10 tbsp)	5 fl oz	150 ml
¾ cup (12 tbsp)	6 fl oz	175 ml
1 cup (16 tbsp)	8 fl oz	250 ml
1¼ cups	10 fl oz	300 ml
1½ cups	12 fl oz	350 ml
1 pint (2 cups)	16 fl oz	500 ml
2½ cups	20 fl oz (1 pint)	625 ml
5 cups	40 fl oz (1 qt)	1.25 L

WEIGHTS

AMERICAN/BRITISH	METRIC
¼ oz	7 g
½ oz	15 g
1 oz	30 g
2 oz	55 g
3 oz	85 g
4 oz (¼ lb)	110 g
5 oz	140 g
6 oz	170 g
7 oz	200 g
8 oz (½ lb)	225 g
9 oz	250 g
10 oz	280 g
11 oz	310 g
12 oz (¾ lb)	340 g
13 oz	370 g
14 oz	400 g
15 oz	425 g
16 oz (1 lb)	450 g

OVEN TEMPERATURES

	°F	°C	GAS MARK
Very cool	250–275	130–140	½–2
Cool	300	148	2
Warm	325	163	3
Medium	350	177	4
Medium hot	375–400	190–204	5–6
Hot	425	218	7
Very hot	450–475	232–245	8–9

RECIPE INDEX

RESTAURANT INDEX